OPPORTUNITIES IN
Music Careers

ROBERT GERARDI

Foreword by
Dr. Billy Taylor
Pianist, Composer, Recording Artist, and Author

VGM Career Books
Chicago New York San Francisco Lisbon London Madrid Mexico City
Milan New Delhi San Juan Seoul Singapore Sydney Toronto

Library of Congress Cataloging-in-Publication Data

Gerardi, Robert.
Opportunities in music careers / Robert Gerardi ; foreword by Billy Taylor.
p. cm. — (VGM opportunities series)
Includes bibliographical references.
ISBN 0-07-138716-1 (hardcover) — ISBN 0-07-138717-X (paperback)
1. Music—Vocational guidance. I. Title. II. Series.

ML3795 .G47 2002
780'.23'73—dc21

2001056861

VGM Career Books

A Division of The ***McGraw·Hill*** *Companies*

1 2 3 4 5 6 7 8 9 0 LBM/LBM 1 0 9 8 7 6 5 4 3 2

ISBN 0-07-138716-1 (hardcover)
ISBN 0-07-138717-X (paperback)

This book was set in Adobe Garamond
Printed and bound by Lake Book Manufacturing

McGraw-Hill books are available at special quantity discounts to use as premiums and sales promotions, or for use in corporate training programs. For more information, please write to the Director of Special Sales, Professional Publishing, McGraw-Hill, Two Penn Plaza, New York, NY 10121-2298. Or contact your local bookstore.

This book is printed on acid-free paper.

Contents

Opportunities in Music Careers is an encyclopedic view of the world of music—pop to classical, performer to management. Its diversity is quite astounding, and a young person in love with music can, with this slim volume, find a place in the field of his or her choice. I was, frankly, surprised by the variety of opportunities in music, and I hope that this becomes required reading for all serious music students.

John Corigliano
Composer, Distinguished Professor; Pulitzer prize winner (2001); Academy Award winner (2000); and Grammy Award winner (1996 and 2000).

Foreword

The music field is an exciting mosaic of unique opportunities. There is a need for innovative, creative, and knowledgeable people in every phase of the business side of this art form.

Most people are attracted to the glamorous and highly visible performance side of the music field, but for a variety of reasons, they end up in management, production, recording, publishing, music education, or other fields in which their musical education and experience can give them an edge.

I am a working musician and, like many of my colleagues, I require a large group of professionals to help me achieve my career goals. I have a management team that books my engagements, a public relations firm that promotes all my various activities, a music business lawyer who advises me on the many legal issues and contracts that govern almost all my activities, and an accountant who helps me keep track of the money I owe and the money owed to me. A record company and a publishing company publish and promote my music, and an investment counselor advises me on the nonmusical investments I make.

This support system gives me a great deal of control over my creative output and enables me to add television, radio, and educational projects to my already crowded schedule, in ways that maximize the use of my time, knowledge, and experience.

Nearly everyone on my support team is a musician or has some background experience in music, and the insights they have developed make them more effective in helping me solve career-related problems. They are resourceful and indispensable to me.

If you are interested and attracted to the broad and diversified field of music, look beyond the performance area and examine the legal, technical, educational, and financial aspects of the apparatus that supports it.

You may find that your strengths, training, and experience not only will establish you as an important contributor to the business end of the music field, but will contribute to your personal development as well.

Reading this book is a very good start.

Dr. Billy Taylor
Pianist, Composer, Recording Artist, and Author

Preface

In writing this book, I had the opportunity to meet many interesting and successful people. I made some new friends and renewed some old friendships. I was able to look back on my own career and draw from my mistakes and successes.

I remember a point in my career when I wanted to work in publishing. One of the largest music publishing companies was looking for a professional manager to run the New York office. I wanted the job very badly.

A friend of mine knew the president of the company and introduced us over the phone. An appointment was set, and we met at the Essex House and had a pleasant conversation. We discussed many things, but I was not offered the job. I left the meeting confused, and it took me a long time to understand why I didn't get the offer. I went to that meeting solely as a musician. I was a singer, a pianist, and a songwriter, but he already knew that. What he was looking for was a corporate executive, a businessperson.

The lesson is this: Had I been prepared with some business and management studies or experience, I would have had something extra to add to that conversation, and I might have gotten that music-publishing job.

Today the music business is becoming more and more complex and competitive, and you've got to meet the challenge.

Whether you're university-trained or the street-fighter brand of musician, you still need experience, and there's only one way to get it: through hard work and preparation. It means trying again and again for that job, working and learning more, and going back again. It's a challenging and rewarding field if you're ambitious, talented, and creative, but you've got to take command and plan your own destiny.

In music, one thing is certain: You will get out of your work what you put into it. Good luck.

Acknowledgments

I WOULD LIKE to thank the following individuals and organizations for their help in making this book possible:

Annette Frank Nolte, music educator and research assistant; Maryann Caputo, editor assistant; Dr. Ron Sadoff, Director of Film Music and Piano Studies, New York University's Steinhardt School of Education; Nancy Shankman, Director of Arts Education, New York City Board of Education; Chief Jack Parker, U.S. Navy Music Program; M.Sgt. Virgil G. Layne, Superintendent, U.S. Air Force Bands; Dr. Bernard Shockett, Chairman, music department, Lehman College; Bill Moriarity, President, Local 802, American Federation of Musicians; John Mahoney, music therapist and Synclavier programmer; Isidro Otis, President, The Clyde Otis Music Group; Steven Stockage, director, screenwriter; Betsy Cecchetti, OPERA America; Jan Wilson, American Symphony Orchestra League; Jon Marcus, Executive Director, National Academy of Recording Arts and Sciences, New York Chapter; C. J.

Williamson, Editor-in-Chief, *Classical Singer Magazine*; Laura Klein and Mark D. Trevino, Meet the Composer.

Special thanks to Jean-Pierre Trebot, Executive Director, New York Friars Club; John Corigliano, Composer, Distinguished Professor, Lehman College/CUNY; Sue Rarus, Music Educators National Conference; Sharon McLoughlin, International Music Products Association (NAMM).

1

The Diverse Field of Music

You just performed at a friend's party, or sang at a local club, and everyone is congratulating you on how good you sound. In fact, someone even says, "What are you doing here? You should be in the big time! You sound as good as the people I've heard on television."

For the first time, you realize that all the years of practice and study have paid off, and you know yourself that you sound as good as some of the professionals. Not only that, but you really enjoy performing. So you make your decision and announce to an unenthusiastic family, "I'm going to become a professional musician." You go to New York or Hollywood, and in two weeks, there you are: a star with your own TV show.

Unfortunately, it's not that easy. If it were, there would be 250 million people with their own TV shows. Everyone would be in the music business. Many people fantasize about conducting Beethoven's Fifth Symphony or singing like Frank Sinatra, Celine Dion, Garth Brooks, Reba McEntire, or another superstar.

Most people see only the tip of the iceberg. They see nothing of the reality behind the fantasy: a network of exciting and lucrative careers that seldom get attention. Dreams of being in the music business are not bad, but it takes hard work and talent to make them come true. A dream without a plan remains a dream. To think that you can step into the spotlight without the necessary training and experience is to give in to delusions of grandeur.

Those who think it is easy to succeed in the music business are in for a big shock. But it also would be unfair to assume that it is impossible to make it. Examine the many diverse careers in music; be aware of the opportunities available as a professional musician. There's much more to the music business than just the bright lights.

Someone has to design and build the musical instruments, tune and repair them, and teach people to play them. The music itself has to be created, arranged and scored, copied and transcribed, and then printed as sheet music. It then has to be published and sold to the public. In order to record the music, musicians, a producer, an engineer, and a recording studio staff must work together to convert the sound into a CD. Each record company has a large marketing staff to distribute recordings to broadcasters and retail stores. Large organizations monitor the sale and performance of the music. Many musicians play music live: a pianist at a house party, a small combo in a cocktail lounge, a dance band, or a large symphony orchestra.

The music business consists of so many levels: from artistic creation to assembly-line production; from spotlight glitter to matter-of-fact business; from managers, lawyers, agents, technicians, and an entire cast of supporting players to a simple country picker singing about a train.

Do You Have What It Takes?

Talent alone is not the key to success in the music business. It takes an aggressive (not to be confused with obnoxious) person to seize important opportunities. And every time you do, you risk rejection. Do you have the courage to stand up and try again? An artist has to have strength and optimism in order to survive.

Rejection can be painful and frustrating. If you let it soak in and take it personally, it can destroy you as an artist and as a person. Do you have confidence in your talents and the conviction to "go for it"? Do you have the humility to know where your weaknesses are and the intelligence to study and work at improving yourself? It's not easy.

Thomas Edison failed thousands of times before he succeeded in inventing the lightbulb. Are you willing to go the extra distance for your success? Do you have the discipline to practice endless hours and study constantly, knowing that you will slide backwards if you falter? Can you tolerate the auditions, the loneliness, the travel, the living away from home, friends, and family? Are you willing to give up your weekends, evenings, and vacations to succeed? Are you ready to accept the fact that even though you're an artist, you must become a businessperson as well?

Show business is filled with stories of superstars who were told that they didn't have it, to go home and give it up. Yet they persisted, and we admire those very people for their professional achievements.

Career Goals and Plans

More than a thousand colleges, universities, conservatories, and specialty schools teach music and music-related subjects. Thousands of students major in composition and instrumental or vocal performance, not to mention those studying music education, music therapy, and music business. Add to that students who study privately and those who are self-taught, and the number of prospective professional musicians is mind-boggling. Each one has the same aspiration: to get a job and make it to the top in an already overcrowded industry.

How do you break into the world of music, overcoming the fierce competition and the overwhelming odds? Not everyone can. Success needs to be measured not by stardom but by the ability to make a living at your chosen profession. Simply surviving in the music business is success in itself.

Getting started in music is no different than it is in any other business. You have to become a working professional and then plan and develop your career. Most beginners, although excellent musicians, are not self-motivated. They tend to think that someone will discover them. Waiting to be discovered is pointless; you have to get up and do it yourself. Gordon Harrell (Broadway conductor and arranger), Yuval Waldman (concert violinist/conductor), and Bert Lucarelli (concert oboist and recording artist) all respond similarly to the question, "How did you make it to where you are?" They explain that they knew exactly what they wanted, they went after it, and everything fell into place. You have to know what you want in order to get it.

First off, develop clear goals. Once you know exactly what you want to do, then you can develop a plan. The plan can consist of learning a repertoire to win a competition or getting a job that will give you the necessary experience, credit, and exposure to move on to your next job. You may need a plan just to survive until something better comes along.

There are two types of people who try to make it in the music business: those who want overnight success and those who are willing to build their careers more slowly. The first group is usually chasing a show-business dream with lots of good intentions and wishful thinking. And they usually fall by the wayside with cliches like, "It's not what you know, but who you know" or "I never get the breaks." Those who seek overnight success want the glamour right away, but they don't understand the hard work required.

Other aspiring musicians build their careers more slowly. They are architects of success, learning how the music business works, discovering what opportunities are available, where to find them, and how to get them. These musicians survive on the lesser jobs, while keeping tuned in to the better ones; they build a network of connections, working as a professional, with professionals, and meeting the right people.

The opportunities in music are so diverse that it is an injustice to have only one objective in mind. You should be willing to step into another music-related career that can keep you in the business. So, begin forming your plan of attack, but make it a flexible, realistic one. Build your career carefully, and you will enjoy a long and successful life in the music industry.

Preparation

You should start your career when you believe you are ready. Your teachers can help you with that decision, but if you're not ready for the professional world, you will be the first to know. Preparing for a career in music takes years of lessons, both practicing and building a repertoire, and it never ends. If you think the preparation is only difficult in the beginning stages of your career, then you are in for a surprise. Once you become a professional, the preparation not only continues, but intensifies. As you develop your career, the competition becomes keener, and you must stay in top shape to meet it. The preparation is both behind you and ahead of you.

You should meet the challenge with curiosity and openness. The more you know, the more you will have to draw on. Be aware of the many different musical styles; look into other areas of the arts, such as painting, sculpture, dance, acting, theater, film, literature, and poetry. Learn the technical and the business aspects of music. Most musicians and singers are multitalented. Develop a variety of skills; besides making you a better performer, these skills may also help you survive.

Survival

Everyone faces good times and bad times in life, but musicians tend to get more than their share of the bad times. At a very early point in your career, you should develop a strong will to survive. Survival sometimes means having to take a couple of steps back before going forward again. During lean periods you may find yourself working in some real dives for little money and little applause, but you can learn a great deal from this experience, continue paying your rent, and be wiser and stronger when a better job comes along. Many of today's concert artists and conductors survived as section players in orchestras until their break came along. Even today's popular singers and musicians survived playing club dates and saloons.

Good Habits

Bill Moriarity, President, Local 802, American Federation of Musicians, told me that club owners and hotel managers look for these characteristics in a musician: punctuality, neat appearance, a pleasant personality, no bad habits, and ability to do the job. Any agent or bandleader would say the same thing. Would you hire a person who was insecure, unhappy, and negative? Would you want to work with a person who was uncooperative, lazy, late for work, and sloppy in appearance?

Good habits will help you build a good reputation and a network of return engagements. Good habits are key to survival in the music field. In the business, creative, and performance end of music, it still takes dependable, conscientious people to get a job done.

Marketing

Knowing where you fit in should be obvious. Do you love classical or jazz, country or rock? Do you enjoy solo work, playing with an ensemble, or do you want to be the leader? Do you prefer studio work, public performance, or composing? Knowing what you want to do will guide your career and drive you toward your long-term goal. Still, you need to survive along the way.

Adjusting your talents for different markets is one way of getting the bread-and-butter work. Learn the style and repertoire to play a cocktail lounge, a club date, or a restaurant. Learn some additional skills in order to work in a record or publishing company. Move to an area that has more opportunities available to you. All of these skills can be part of your survival strategy.

Promotion

Promoting yourself means making your talents known. Even the biggest stars need constant promotion to keep both the industry and the public aware of them. A record album, a concert, a television special, or a movie all require promotion in order to succeed. Established entertainers pay large sums of money to press agents and public relations firms to keep their names in the public eye.

As the laws of physics state, for every action there is a reaction. The action of promoting causes the reaction of interest. Cause enough interest, and opportunities will begin to open up to you.

You might have all the talent in the world, but unless you tell someone about it, you're just singing in the shower. The technique of self-promotion involves having a bag of tricks, or the tools with which to make friends and attract attention.

The Inside Tools

The inside tools for getting started are confidence, personality, and a positive attitude. Don't underestimate the importance of that statement. If you are a happy person and love music, it will show. If you don't love music, you're in the wrong business.

You will also need a good sense of humor. In order to survive the pressures of the music business, you'll have to know how to laugh at it, and sometimes at yourself. Another important tool is supportive friends, relatives, associates, and teachers. It is hard to develop a career in music when surrounded by negativity, doubt, fear, and superstition.

The Outside Tools

In addition to the right attitude and personality, an aspiring musician needs some basic business tools to launch a career. These include business cards, a résumé, photographs, flyers, postcards, a press kit, demos, and an answering machine or service. Once you have these basic tools of self-promotion, you will need to use them in combination with a system of networking, auditioning, and making the rounds to look for jobs. Some young performers look for places to showcase their talent or set up debut recitals. These are the outside tools for starting your career in music.

Business Cards

A business card should be simple, elegant, and straightforward. It should list your name, your talent, and a telephone number or E-mail address where you can be reached. An address is optional. Since this card is to represent you, it should be the highest quality you can afford. It might be wise to consider artwork, a logo, color, or special type, so that your card will stand out from those of your competitors.

The Telephone

The telephone is probably the most important instrument you'll ever use. It has the power to open doors, and it lets you introduce yourself and make appointments. You can talk to an agent or a producer in Los Angeles, New York, or anywhere in the world.

Before you start to run up an expensive printing bill for business cards, be sure you have a permanent phone number. Some people like to have an answering service and use that number on their cards. That way, each time you change your address and phone number, your stationery won't be affected. It is very unprofessional to have a phone that doesn't answer, or one that's answered by a kid sister, a grandfather, or a roommate groping for a pencil. If you live with other people, get a separate business phone number and have a pickup service, voice mail, or a phone answering machine.

The Résumé

Your résumé should be well planned and carefully laid out. The reader should be able to use it as a road map of your career.

First and foremost, give your name, address, telephone number, and your affiliation with any professional organizations (such as unions or guilds). Membership in these organizations establishes you immediately as a working professional. Next, indicate your main talent, your instrument (violin, trumpet, piano), or voice and range.

Then list your most important and impressive credits, starting with the most recent and working backward. Also indicate any competitions, awards, or scholarships you have won, and describe your training—formal and private. Finally, mention any notable special abilities such as second instruments, composing, arranging, copying, or transcribing.

The résumé should be neat, easy to read, and honest. Don't fill it with items that waste the reader's time. Above all, be truthful. One false statement and the validity of your whole résumé is threatened.

Since most musicians and singers are multitalented, you may need several versions of your résumé, each emphasizing a different specialty. Perhaps you're a singer whose main objective is opera, but you also make a living singing religious music; then you should have two résumés. One résumé would present the religious credits and repertoire first, and the other would stress the opera career.

VGM Career Books publishes *How to Write a Winning Résumé*, a book that explains how to put together a résumé and compose a cover letter. Also, the Superintendent of Documents has a catalog available that lists the pamphlet *Résumés, Application Forms, Cover*

Letters, and Interviews. The pamphlet explains how to prepare a résumé, write a letter of application, and have a successful interview. The pamphlet costs $2.00, and the catalog is available for free by writing to the Consumer Information Center, Dept. 107C, Pueblo, CO 81002; pueblo.gsa.gov, 1-888-878-3256.

If you can afford it, consider using a good quality paper when having your résumé reproduced. Stationery is also something to consider. It is professional to have cover letters and envelopes imprinted with a letterhead on quality paper. If your budget will allow, a little flash won't hurt.

Photographs

Photographs are another important tool for promoting yourself. Your 8-by-10-inch glossy should be taken by a professional photographer and should be a good likeness of yourself. It should convey warmth and personality, so that whoever looks at it will want to meet you or, better yet, hire you. You may also want to have some photos of yourself in performance.

Flyers

A flyer is an advertisement that can be mailed to anyone you believe is important to your career. It should contain your name; the place, time, and date of your engagement; and your picture. Depending upon your budget, it can be simply designed and printed on a computer, or it can incorporate some artwork, have typeset text, and be prepared by a printer.

Postcards

Postcards, preferably with your picture on one side, can be very effective. Use them as a flyer or as a follow-up to a flyer or performance. A postcard is a sure way of getting your face, name, and message onto someone's desk. Think of yourself as a product that has to be packaged and advertised. Repetition and persistence are needed to sell a product.

Press Kit

Think of a press kit (or portfolio) as a do-it-yourself kit. It's a package of all the publicity from past performances. A press kit can be a collage of newspaper clippings, advertisements, reviews, write-ups, flyers, and programs. As in the résumé, the most impressive and most recent credits should be up front.

The press kit should be entertaining and informative and should be more than just a bunch of copies stapled together. It takes careful planning and a good eye to create an interesting layout and presentation.

In order to build a press kit, you need to have something to put in it. Try to get some form of coverage for each engagement. Inviting the local press, making sure that each booking is advertised in the local newspaper, and sending out flyers are all effective forms of promotion.

Your press kit can be presented in a plastic or paper folder, the type that can be purchased in any good stationery store. If your budget allows, the kit can be bound with your name imprinted on the cover.

Demo

The demo, short for demonstration record, is a good way to audition, especially for a job that's far from your home. There are two types of demos: audio and video. Although the cassette audiotape is still popular and easy to use, the CD format is becoming the choice of musicians and the industry. A home CD burner makes it easy to transfer your demo onto a CD, and your computer can print out CD labels making it look neat, organized (there are label programs available for the computer), and professional.

The demo, like the résumé and press kit, should be well planned. It should be short, entertaining, and include a variety of your best performances. A demo can be recorded at home, at a live performance, or in a studio. Although it is more expensive to do a demo in a professional recording studio, the difference may be worth it. The more professional the recording, the better you will sound.

The video demo is also becoming a popular means of auditioning talent. There are three types of video formats: VHS, ¾-inch professional cassette, and the DVD format, which is becoming more popular and accessible. Although the DVD can be recorded in your home studio, it is still very expensive as compared to the VHS format.

Ask which format the agent or producer uses. Many agents and producers have access to all of these formats, but they might prefer to view a performer's video at their own convenience in the comfort and privacy of their office or home.

Networking

Networking means meeting the right people. The best way to get to know other musicians, singers, and writers is through professional organizations. Unions, guilds, and associations all have members with a shared interest in music. Attend meetings, seminars, and workshops; get involved in their activities and special projects, all of which will afford you the opportunity to meet people in the music business.

Showcase clubs are another good place to meet people. If you have talent and an open personality, it shouldn't be hard to make friends. The trade papers or a local entertainment directory should have a list of showcase clubs. The yellow pages list record companies, publishing companies, and agents. Making the rounds and meeting people is the best way to build connections.

Every audition or job gives you a chance to meet people who can give you advice and help in building your career. Doing a good job will help you get recommended for other work. And, in turn, you can recommend other people for jobs. It's all a matter of getting into the inner circle and building a reputation and a good relationship with other working professionals.

Rounds

When an artist makes rounds, he or she is like a salesperson going from door to door with a product. The artist faces the same challenge, and the same possible rejection, as any other salesperson. However, since the artist is both the salesperson and the product, he or she must do all the work alone.

First of all, a campaign strategy must be planned out. Start with a list of names, addresses, and phone numbers of anyone you think you need to know: agents, managers, record company executives, publishers, and club owners. Make phone calls to introduce yourself and make appointments. Develop a good phone technique, and keep accurate records of each call. If they ask you to call back in three days, or tell you not to call again, you need to follow up the conversation appropriately.

Learn how to be persistent without being a pest. A phone call can be followed by a mailing, a picture and résumé, a follow-up letter, a flyer, or a postcard. Managers, agents, and executives are very busy people and don't generally see anyone without an appointment. However, they do have good memories and will remember your name and recognize the fact that you were knocking on their door. Eventually, your persistence will be noticed.

Auditions

An audition is a job application, and you must demonstrate your talent. In most cases, there isn't enough time to give an extensive example of your work, so you must plan carefully and select material that shows your best qualities in a very short time.

Many singers and musicians get overly ambitious and try to tackle material that's not right for them. This is a mistake. Even superstars have to audition for a movie or a Broadway play, and the audition material must be suited to both the performer and the particular audition.

A career in music is also a career in job hunting; learning how to audition and how to enjoy auditioning is a giant step in the right direction. It's important to have a good attitude, a good personality, confidence, and to love what you are doing. All of this will show at the audition. Actor/singer Len Cariou, who has starred in numerous films and Broadway plays and who won a Tony Award for his performance in the Broadway musical *Sweeney Todd*, gives this advice to young aspiring performers when auditioning: be prepared, relaxed, confident, and above all, learn to enjoy the experience.

Not getting the job does not mean your performance was bad. In most cases it simply means that the producers or directors were looking for a different type of performer. It's important to come away from the audition happy and satisfied that you did a good job. The way you feel about yourself and your work has a great effect on the quality of future performances; therefore, you must have a positive attitude. A string of good auditions is guaranteed to get you a job sooner or later.

Showcases

In the early days of vaudeville, the audience booed, hissed, and threw vegetables at the entertainer if they didn't like the act. Someone backstage would administer the final blow by dragging the entertainer off the stage with a big hook.

Today, the showcase stage is tough, like the stages of vaudeville. And even though we're too civilized for vegetables and hooks, the audience still determines each performer's fate. Every performance is a showcase, and the next project and connection depend on the previous performance. For example, you may be working in one club and invite the owner of another club to sample your work for possible future engagements.

The showcase is a much misunderstood concept. In recent years it has come to mean free music, and many club owners have taken advantage of young talent in need of a place to perform. These clubs serve expensive drinks while the acts work for little or no pay. The audience consists of people the performers invited themselves, by using their own money to print and mail flyers advertising the performance. Still, this format is an important part of beginning a career in music. A singer or musician can use a showcase to her or his advantage. A showcase allows performers to break in an act; try out new material in front of a live audience; and invite agents, club owners, managers, and the press.

Many entertainers get caught up in the showcase syndrome and end up doing it just for the applause. At the same time, many entertainers have been discovered in showcase clubs and have moved on to become celebrities, or at least have gained the experience necessary to become working professionals.

Recitals

Many soloists come to New York to get national recognition as a concert artist. After a period of freelancing, knocking on doors, and auditioning, they may decide to present themselves in a debut recital. It's a risky and expensive proposition, but some have made it work to their advantage.

To give a recital, you have to rent a hall, advertise, give every friend and relative a ticket, and invite arts managers who generally don't like to attend these kinds of recitals. If you are studying with a well-respected teacher whose word is highly regarded, the managers may show up.

Reviewers are the most important people to invite since a favorable press review can gain the interest of the arts managers. An unfavorable review may cause some people to run from the business. Others just study more, practice harder, continue working, and try it all over again.

2

The Serious Performer

Orchestras

According to the American Symphony Orchestra League, there are more than 1,800 symphony orchestras in this country that employ full-time, part-time, and student musicians. Symphony orchestras can be divided into three categories: (1) orchestras with expenses in excess of $1 million, (2) orchestras with expenses between $260,000 and $1 million, and (3) orchestras with expenses less than $260,000. There are approximately 103 orchestras in the first category, 101 in the second, and 1,030 orchestras in the third category. (The remainder is made up of amateur orchestras.) The 40 largest orchestras collectively employ more than 3,500 musicians in a season. Large orchestras employ 85 to 105 players, while smaller ones employ 60 to 75 players. Some players are paid on a contract basis with a yearly salary, vacation, and benefits; others are hired on a per-performance basis.

Rehearsal and performance schedules can be very demanding. For example, in one season the New York Philharmonic reported 157 performances; the Boston Symphony Orchestra, 277; the Chicago Symphony Orchestra, 185; the Philadelphia Symphony Orchestra, 192; the Pittsburgh Symphony Orchestra, 170; the Cincinnati Symphony Orchestra, 138; the Cleveland Symphony Orchestra, 186; the Los Angeles Philharmonic, 239; the San Francisco Symphony Orchestra, 941; the Detroit Symphony Orchestra, 230; and the Minnesota Symphony Orchestra, 180. A season runs from 29 to 52 weeks, with 24 orchestras guaranteeing a 52-week season.

Salaries of musicians in symphony orchestras range from $842 to $1,760 per week; however, according to the American Federation of Musicians, earnings in major orchestras ranged from about $21,000 to $95,000 annually during the 1998–99 season. Each orchestra works out a separate contract with the AFM's union local. Salaries are not as high for regional orchestras because they have fewer performances. Musicians who work a short season have to find ways of supplementing their incomes. Those who work on a per-performance basis usually receive a prorated salary. A wage scale chart is available from the American Federation of Musicians, 1501 Broadway, New York, NY 10036; afm.org.

Most orchestras prefer the standard works of classical composers. Therefore, a musician should be familiar with the standard repertoire. There are, however, some orchestras that specialize in performing twentieth-century compositions.

Orchestral Training

Musicianship among orchestra members is of the highest caliber, and ability to read music is essential. Being able to work well with a large group and to follow directions is very important. A musician generally starts studying at a very early age, and after many years of private instruction he or she should also study at a university or conservatory. Studying with a performer in a major symphony can be very important to a younger musician's career.

Constant ensemble work and experience are necessary to qualify for a symphony orchestra. There are many college orchestras to train with, as well as summer workshops. Teachers and schools often have information that can help you find these workshops and positions with orchestras.

The National Federation of Music Clubs publishes a guide to scholarships and awards. It lists categories and requirements for scholarships from the various colleges and universities that offer summer workshops.

Also, major symphony orchestras offer educational programs, orchestral training opportunities, student competitions, master classes, and fellowships. For example, the Boston Symphony Orchestra has the "Tanglewood" concert series in the summer, bso.org; the New York Philharmonic offers a "Young Artists Competition," nyphilharmon.org; the Philadelphia Orchestra offers "Master Classes" and "Student Competitions," philorch.org; the Los Angeles Philharmonic offers a "Young Artists Competition," laphil.org; the Cleveland Orchestra has a "Youth Orchestra," clevelandorch.com; and so forth. You can locate and find information about an orchestra near you online.

Finding Jobs

Openings for musicians in symphony orchestras can be found in the back of *International Musician*, the official journal of the American Federation of Musicians. The July 2001 issue advertised 169 openings for various instruments in 48 different orchestras. *International Musician* also lists ads for scholarships, fellowships, competitions, and seminars. You should consider subscribing to the journal. For information write to *International Musician*, 1501 Broadway, New York, NY 10036; afm.org.

The American Symphony Orchestra League has available to its members the bimonthly publication, *Symphony Magazine*, and four E-mail services that provide valuable and timely information: "In the News," "From the Field," "On the Move," and "At the League." It also offers graduate courses through the orchestra Leadership Academy for orchestra administration and the National Conducting Institute for conductors. In addition there is an online job and résumé search service.

If you are considering moving to another part of the country, you should also read the local union newsletter.

Openings are often found by word of mouth; therefore, being in the orchestra system is the best way of finding work.

To apply for a position, you must send a résumé and, in some cases, a tape. If the audition is far away from your home, you may have to pay for your own travel expenses. Auditions are held behind a screen, so that no prejudices will enter into the judgment.

Supplemental Work

Most musicians who work in major symphony, opera, or ballet orchestras spend their entire careers in one position. That makes for a very tight job market. Sometimes up to ninety hopefuls will apply for one position. Many symphony musicians also play in smaller chamber orchestras, which advertise openings in *International Musician* as well. Chamber Music America, 305 Seventh Avenue, New York, NY 10001, chamber-music.org, is another good source of leads. It publishes a quarterly magazine, *Chamber Music*; a membership directory; and *The Directory of Summer Chamber Music Workshops. Musical America Directory of the Performing Arts* has a complete list of symphony and chamber orchestras; musicalamerica.com.

Many symphonic musicians perform in solo recitals or in duos, trios, quartets, and ensembles. Many private affairs and restaurants will hire a classical string quartet or a harpist, sometimes alternating with a dance band. Check with local contractors and club date bandleaders who book music for private affairs.

In one year in the United States, six thousand students graduated with degrees in performance. In that same year, there were about four hundred openings in symphony orchestras. A young musician generally has to become part of the freelance pool to earn a living and has to frequently audition while waiting for a break. It often takes from three to five years of living in near poverty for a young musician to get that break. And there are no guarantees. Luck, timing, and politics all play important parts in establishing yourself.

Positions Available

In addition to the actual players, each orchestra offers many behind-the-scenes positions that need to be filled: general manager, assistant manager, public relations director, fund-raising coordinator. There are jobs for musicians as well, such as librarian or stage manager. If you are studying with a symphony musician, you might try to work at one of those jobs until a back chair opens up. A knowledge of business and management might be an asset. For most of these jobs, you may have to be a member of the American Federation of Musicians. Information on developing a career in orchestra administration as well as conducting is available at the American Symphony Orchestra League's website: symphony.org.

Instruments

These are the instruments of the orchestra:

- *Strings*: violin, viola, cello, double bass
- *Woodwinds*: piccolo, flute, oboe, English horn, clarinet, bass clarinet, bassoon, contrabassoon
- *Brass*: French horn, trumpet, trombone, tuba
- *Percussion*: piano, kettledrums, celesta, glockenspiel, xylophone, bells, triangle, tambourine, snare, bass drum, cymbals, gong, and others
- *Harp*

The ability to play other instruments related to your main instrument can be a valuable asset in getting work with orchestras. Also, playing in studios and musical theater requires the ability to double—that is, to play more than one instrument. In fact, some musicians have switched instruments several times before finding their niche.

Solo Concert Performers

The career of a concert artist begins at a very early age. Studying with a highly qualified teacher who can recognize and develop the qualities of virtuosity—and guide your career—is essential. Although a young musician may have studied privately for many years developing technique and repertoire, a university or conservatory education still is extremely important. The high level of training, the energy of the school environment, and the constant exposure to other equally talented students will provide the fine tuning necessary for the concert artist.

It is important to work with teachers who inspire your playing and allow you to grow into your own style and identity. A teacher whose reputation is respected in the arts management field also can be very helpful in getting your career off to a good start.

In order to get into the system of the concert performance, you must be self-motivated and totally committed. You must do everything you can to get exposure and experience. You must seek out the competitions that will get you a scholarship to a conservatory in order to obtain recognition as a concert artist.

It is very rare for anyone without a formal education to succeed in the concert field. Talent scouts are everywhere: teachers, administrators, and arts managers. A competition can win you a recital sponsored by an important association or guild. That, in turn, can win you a favorable press review and recognition from an arts manager with a contract for a concert tour. Competitions, grants, awards, scholarships, arts managers, and supportive organizations are listed in *Musical America, International Directory of the Performing Arts*, musicalamerica.com; and *Sterns Performing Arts Directory*, dancemagazine.com.

A concert might pay you $1,000 or more. That doesn't include room and board, travel, or agent commissions. What seems like a lot of money really isn't. You'll have to find a way of supplementing your income until the money gets better.

Be sure that you are willing to live out of a suitcase before you choose the concert circuit as your career goal. A successful concert artist sometimes does sixty to one hundred concerts a year. That adds up to a great deal of traveling.

However, the performance and the traveling are only part of it. You may have played a beautiful concerto, but the final show for approval is at the cocktail reception afterward. Can you socialize? Do you enjoy meeting and talking with people? A good personality is very important to a successful concert career. Many concert artists make guest appearances with symphony orchestras. Concert artists also teach privately and are on staff with conservatories, colleges, and universities. Strong interpersonal skills are important in each of these situations.

Organizations to Contact

Concert solo instruments are generally limited to piano, violin, cello, organ, harp, guitar, horns, woodwinds, and voice. Concert ensembles include two pianos, harp ensembles, string quartets, woodwind and brass ensembles. The Concert Artists Guild presents soloists and ensembles in a debut recital with press coverage. For audition information write to Concert Artists Guild, Inc., 850 Seventh Avenue, Suite 1205, New York, NY 10019, concert artists.org.

The Interlochen Center for the Arts, P.O. Box 199, Interlochen, MI 49643-0199, interlochen.org, offers young musicians the opportunity of intensive study in summer workshop programs.

Young Concert Artists is a nonprofit management organization that encourages outstanding young solo musicians and helps launch their careers. For audition information write to Young Concert Artists, Inc., 250 West 57th Street, New York, NY 10019, yca.org.

Young Musicians Foundation encourages young musicians in the Southwest by offering them performance opportunities and financial assistance. For information and application, write to Young Musicians Foundation, 195 South Beverly Drive, Beverly Hills, CA 90212, ymf.org.

Other organizations that may provide you with helpful information include the following:

American Federation of Musicians
1501 Broadway
New York, NY 10036
afm.org

American Symphony Orchestra League
33 West Sixtieth Street, 5th Floor
New York, NY 10023-7905
symphony.org

Chamber Music America
305 Seventh Avenue
New York, NY 10001
chamber-music.org

National Federation of Music Clubs
1336 North Delaware Street
Indianapolis, IN 46202
nfmc-music.org

National Youth Orchestra of Canada
1032 Bathurst Street
Toronto, ON M5R-3G7
Canada
nyoc.org

Opera

Opera is an art form that combines voice (solo and chorus), theater, ballet, and a symphony orchestra with old world traditions and new world technology in a grand performance, a performance that finishes to standing ovations.

OPERA America has a membership of 134 opera companies: 117 in 44 states, and 17 in 5 Canadian provinces. They also have 37 affiliated international companies in 20 countries in Europe, Australia, Asia, and South America. OPERA America companies had a collective budget of $650 million and employed more than 20,000 people on a full-time and part-time basis, as of the most recent survey.

According to the National Endowment for the Arts, audiences for opera grew by almost 25 percent between 1982 and 1992, and opera's share of the total arts audience grew by 12.5 percent, more than any other art form. In terms of demographics opera audiences tend to be older, more wealthy, highly educated, and live in the suburbs, with the median age at 44 (in a 1997 survey). Youthful audiences (18 to 35) have increased by 18 percent.

OPERA America publishes the following guides and directories: *Career Guide for Singers*, 5th edition; *Career Guide Update* (bimonthly); Perspectives Series: "Making Choices: From Classroom to Contracts," "Business Advice for Singers," "Audition Advice for Singers," "The Singer/Manager Relationship"; *Voices*; *Directory of Opera Education Programs*; *Directory of American and Foreign Contemporary Operas and Musical Theater Works 1980–1990* (Central Opera Service, 1990); and *OPERA America Register of Members*. For membership application, information, price, and ordering publications: OPERA America, 1156

Fifteenth Street NW, Suite 810, Washington, D.C. 20005-1704, operaam.org.

According to the National Endowment for the Arts, opera, like symphony and chamber orchestras, is subsidized by foundations and grants. A survey of 331 opera, symphony, and chamber companies showed that 40 percent of the costs were defrayed by the price of admission and 60 percent were covered by foundations; corporations; private contributions; and city, state, and federal funding.

In one season the Metropolitan Opera produced 20 to 25 operas in 265 performances, and the San Francisco Opera produced 14 operas in 75 regular performances and 16 spring performances. Smaller companies produce only three or four operas in a season.

Opera, whether grand or lyric (light), tragic or comic, takes the combined talents of singers, musicians, dancers, conductors, prompters, stage directors, choreographers, vocal coaches, accompanists, stage managers, librarians, makeup artists, hairstylists, scenic designers, set builders, property managers, costume designers, wardrobe managers, and lighting specialists.

Smaller opera companies hire well-known singers to perform the principal roles, and that makes it very difficult for young singers to get leading parts. Singers who are starting a career in opera should seek out competitions, apprenticeship programs, chorus work, and workshops. The competition is very intense. Working and studying in Europe is a good way to gain experience, exposure, and repertoire. Working in a chorus is steady and may give you a chance to perform a minor part. Much can be learned from watching a star perform, and being in the chorus as part of the performance is a great advantage.

The top pay scale for a chorus singer in 2000–01 was approximately $1,100 per week and for a principle singer $1,400 per week. These numbers vary according to the size of the opera company, its location, number of performances, and size of the role. There are also rehearsal pay and media payment for radio and television broadcasts, as well as CD and videocassettes (if recorded). An opera star would be paid more than scale.

Operatic Training

Aspiring opera singers should begin general music studies at an early age; their vocal training should begin at a more mature age, usually in the teens, and will continue throughout their careers. A good background in music, foreign languages, and piano is very important.

Besides a private voice teacher to help develop technique, a singer also needs to study with a vocal coach to develop a repertoire. A singer is a musician whose instrument is the voice. Like a concert instrumentalist, he or she should seek out a formal education and studies in language, sight-singing, harmony, and theory, as well as coaching in early Italian art songs, German lieder, and English and French art songs. Operas are written in Italian, French, English, German, Russian, and Czech. An opera singer usually speaks more than one language and should be familiar with several others. Dance, acting, and other theater skills are also necessary. Opera workshops, vocal ensemble, and solo recitals are all part of the preparation for a career in opera.

Female singers are classified as soprano, mezzo-soprano, and contralto. Men are classified as countertenor, tenor, baritone, and bass (basso). Further classifications are coloratura, lyric, spinto, robusto, dramatic, and basso profundo.

A singer must have a good-quality voice, good intonation, diction, phrasing, musicality, and style, as well as a technique that displays vocal control, agility, and dynamics. A singer must also possess stage presence, charisma, and the ability to work well with others and follow directions. Most importantly, a singer must have patience. A voice that is pushed before its time can end a career before it starts. A singer should know his or her voice and concentrate on developing the repertoire that shows off its style and ability.

Finding Teachers, Grants, and Scholarships

The Metropolitan National Council sponsors an audition program seeking potential talent for the future. There are sixteen regions in the United States and Canada, each divided into districts. The age requirements are 19 to 33 for women and 20 to 33 for men. The applicant must be able to sing five arias in more than one language. The finals are held at the Metropolitan Opera at Lincoln Center, in New York. Winners receive grants to further their studies, as well as valuable exposure and credibility. For more details write to the Metropolitan Opera National Council, Lincoln Center, New York, NY 10023, metopera.org.

The National Association of Teachers of Singing (NATS) is an organization made up of approximately fifty-eight hundred voice teachers throughout the country. Rules for joining NATS are strict, and its teacher members adhere to a code of ethics.

NATS sponsors an artists' competition that awards a $10,000 first prize and thirteen additional prizes for finalists and semifinalists. An applicant may or may not be a professional, but he or she must have studied with a NATS teacher for at least two years. The competition starts at a district level, goes to fourteen regional levels, and then goes to the finals, which are held every two years (in July) at the NATS convention.

The *Journal of Singing* is available to members and nonmembers and is published five times a year. It contains articles on voice and opera, voice pedagogy, and book, music, and record reviews. For subscription information and a list of NATS teachers, write to: The National Association of Teachers of Singing, 6406 Merrill Road, Suite B, Jacksonville, FL 32277, nats.org.

New York Singing Teachers Association (NYSTA) is similar to NATS, except that it concentrates on singers in the New York area. Most singing teachers in and around New York belong to both NYSTA and NATS. NYSTA also has a "Teacher Certification Program," and its goal is "Educating the Voice Teacher of Tomorrow."

NYSTA provides an essential forum for exchanging ideas about the principles of good singing and the practices of good teaching. General meetings are held monthly from October through May and feature leading figures in vocal performance, interpretation, pedagogy, and health. NYSTA also sponsors lectures and panel discussions, master classes, student competitions, awards and recitals, an annual composers' concert, an annual luncheon honoring an outstanding American singer, and hands-on workshops on pedagogy, voice science, and body work. For information contact the New York Singing Teachers Association, nysta.org.

Singers working in opera usually belong to the American Guild of Musical Artists (1727 Broadway, New York, NY 10019-5214, musicalartists.org). Singers working in musical theater usually belong to Actors' Equity Association (165 West 46th Street, New York, NY 10036, actorsequity.org).

The American Institute of Musical Studies (AIMS) presents the AIMS Graz Experience each year in Graz, Austria. This includes the Summer Vocal Institute, the AIMS Chorale, and the AIMS Graz Festival Orchestra. Advertisements are placed in *Opera News* (operanews.com), *Musical America* (musicalamerica.com), *Opera Canada* (dvtail.com), and *International Musician* (afm.org), as well as in other trade journals. Auditions are held for singers, pianists, and instrumentalists. AIMS also sponsors seminars, master classes, and workshops in the United States. For further information and to be placed on the mailing list, write to AIMS, 6621 Snider Plaza, Dallas, TX 75205, www.aimsgraz.org.

Another good source of information for auditions, competitions, and training opportunities is *Classical Singer Magazine*. This is a monthly magazine and online publication that features interviews with famous singers, who give advice to young singers; addresses union and legal issues; and provides up-to-the-minute E-mail notices of auditions. It includes a directory of vocal coaches, accompanists, and voice teachers. There is also a directory of forums in more than six hundred colleges and universities and a summer programs directory. For subscription information contact *Classical Singers Magazine*, P.O. Box 278, Maplewood, NJ 07040, classicalsinger.com.

Conductors

A conductor is a total musician whose instrument is the orchestra. Singers can take a deep breath and let out a song, instrumentalists can pick up their instruments and make music, but the conductor must have an orchestra to lead.

Standing on a podium in front of a symphony orchestra is a thrilling experience. Taking leadership of a hundred personalities and temperaments and directing them according to one interpretation of the music requires great strength. A conductor must have a good personality, leadership skills, and charisma. In addition to command and technique of the baton, a conductor must have an excellent sense of rhythm, a good ear, a knowledge of all the orchestral instruments, a large repertoire, and a good feel for all of the music styles.

A knowledge of the piano is important in order to work on scores, and playing an orchestral instrument affords the conductor the chance to be part of an orchestra as a musician, and also to learn from within. Many famous conductors started their careers as string players, assistant conductors, or concert master.

For example, accomplished concert violinist and conductor Yuval Waldman started his career as a section player in an orchestra, studied at conservatories both here and in Europe, worked his way up to Concert Master of the Kansas City Philharmonic, and from there went on to become a concert violinist (soloist) and conductor.

Yuval explains that it is important for a conductor to spend some time as a member of an orchestra so that he or she can get to know the orchestra from the inside—to understand its psychology. A conductor must also become familiar with the string section, since the strings are the heart and soul of the orchestra.

Training

A conductor usually starts studying at an early age, learning an instrument and the basics of music. University or conservatory training is essential. A school with a good orchestra and many smaller groups can give a student much experience at conducting.

There are many competitions for conductors, and getting exposure can lead to acceptance in a conductor-training program. Competitions are listed in *Musical America: International Directory of the Performing Arts*, musicalamerica.com.

There are thousands of orchestras, both national and international. Some offer apprenticeships and positions as assistant conductors. Opera and ballet companies, musical theater, Broadway and Off-Broadway shows, regional companies, dinner theaters, and summer stock all have orchestras that need conductors. *The Chronicle of Higher Education* (1255 Twenty-third Street NW, Washington, D.C. 20037) has a classified section with ads seeking conductors to fill vacancies with college and university orchestras.

Conductors compose, arrange, and orchestrate. Many jobs need the services of a multitalented conductor who can write and accompany singers in rehearsal. A conductor or musical director must wear many hats. Besides the obvious demands on talent and leadership, he or she must also be able to manage the orchestra's business affairs, helping to plan the budget, scheduling programs, hosting visiting artists, and socializing at cocktail parties. Fundraising is a very important part of the job. Every orchestra needs money to function, and the conductor, being the focal point of the orchestra, must have a warm and open personality in order to attract these funds.

Working as an opera coach can give a conductor the chance to learn the repertoire and get the experience of conducting for a small opera company. Eventually a conductor can work his or her way up to an assistantship in a light opera company or musical theater company.

Conductors can also find work in churches and synagogues as choir directors. And there are many community and school projects that require the services of a good choral director.

Some conductors travel as guest conductors, and others stay with one orchestra. Salaries can range from about $10,000 to more than $100,000 a year. That includes recordings and guest appearances with other orchestras.

Getting the right exposure is important in getting an arts manager to sign a conductor. When conductors are seasoned and ready, they sometimes hire a hall and an orchestra in New York, invite the press, and present themselves in a debut performance.

Musical Theater

The musical theater requires the same high caliber musician as do the symphony and the opera. In fact, many Broadway pit musicians are, or have been, members of a symphony and/or opera orchestra. The musical producer hires a contractor, who in turn hires the musicians. Knowing the contractor can be advantageous when trying to get work in a pit orchestra.

Theatrical Index (Price-Berkley Publication, 888 Eighth Avenue, New York, NY 10019), theatricalindex@nyc.rr.com) maintains a list of future productions, along with the names, addresses, and phone numbers of the producers, as well as the director, composer, librettist, and musical director. It lists the Broadway and Off-Broadway productions, the national companies, and the tours. Musicians, singers, conductors, arrangers, and orchestrators alike should find this weekly publication very useful. It is available by subscription or single issue.

Regional theater has grown throughout the country and has opened up many opportunities for composers and performing artists. Actors' Equity Association (AEA) maintains a list of regional theaters (LORT) and summer theaters. The *Screen and Stage* directory also contains information on summer and regional theaters (Peter Glenn Publications, pgdirect.com).

Additional Organizations

Other helpful organizations include the following:

American Harp Society
P.O. Box 38334
Los Angeles, CA 90038-0334
harpsociety.org

Conductors Guild, Inc.
North Lakeside Cultural Center
6219 North Sheridan Road
Chicago, IL 60660-1729
www.conductorsguild.org

Professional Women Singers Association, Inc.
P.O. Box 884
Planetarium Station
New York, NY 10024
pwsa.homestead.com

Robert Hansen National Opera Association
P.O. Box 60869
Canyon, TX 79016-0869
noa.org

3

The Music Creator

The Composer

Writing serious music today is a difficult way to make a living. Few composers of serious contemporary music earn a living strictly as composers. There are, however, foundations that give grants and awards to composers.

A good source of information on foundations is the Foundation Center. There are more than fifty-nine thousand active foundations in the United States. There are two Foundation national libraries and two Foundation field offices in the United States. The Foundation Center also has available publications and supplemental resources, on CD-ROM, to cooperating collections in more than two hundred public, university, government, and foundation libraries in all fifty states, Australia, Canada, Mexico, Puerto Rico, the Virgin Islands, Great Britain, and Japan. Go to fdncenter.org on the Web to find the collection nearest you.

One good source of grants is the National Endowment for the Arts (NEA). In one year, the NEA music program received a total of 1,766 applications and awarded 756 grants totaling slightly more than 12 million dollars. The grants went to orchestras; chamber, new music, and jazz ensembles; choruses; composers; and music festivals. In the same year, the NEA awarded two hundred grants, totaling 4.2 million dollars, to opera-musical theater for new American works. However, due to past Congressional cutbacks and changes, the music program has been dropped, and grants are no longer available to individuals but are available to nonprofit organizations. Literature and applications can be obtained from: NEA, 1100 Pennsylvania Avenue NW, Washington, D.C. 20506-0001, www.arts.gov.

Meet the Composer, the nation's premier composer service organization, was founded in 1974 to foster the creation, performance, and recording of music by American composers, and to develop new audiences for contemporary music. Meet the Composer raises money from foundations, corporations, individual patrons, and government sources, and designs programs that support all styles of music from folk, ethnic, jazz, electronic, symphonic, and chamber to choral, music theater, opera, and dance. MTC awards grants for composer fees to nonprofit organizations that perform, present, or commission original works.

MTC programs include Meet the Composer Fund, Music Alive, New Residencies, Commissioning Music/USA, Compose Yourself, and the Meet the Composer Fund for Small Ensembles. Publications include: *Commissioning Music*, *Volunteer Lawyers for the Arts Guide to Copyright for Musicians and Composers*, *Composer in Residence: Meet the Composer Residencies Program*, and *Composer/Choreographer Commissioning Handbook*. For information write to:

Meet the Composer, Inc., 2112 Broadway, Suite 505, New York, NY 10023, meetthecomposer.org.

The American Society of Composers, Authors and Publishers (ASCAP) and Broadcast Music, Inc. (BMI) also award grants to composers. There are many organizations and associations that promote and encourage new composers. *Music America International Directory of Performing Arts* lists grants, awards, and competitions. Your local public library should have a copy. *Sterns Performing Arts Directory* is another source of information.

A composer is the creative force in music and must have a good imagination and understanding of the emotional effects of music. A thorough knowledge of harmony and theory, familiarity with sounds and ranges of instruments, and an understanding of the techniques of composing and arranging are essential. Composers write symphony and chamber music, opera, choral music, church music, ballet, and theater music; they also write for commercials, industrials, feature films, and television. Composers create everything from band music to jingles to popular music.

Teaching in a college, university, or conservatory is one of the best sources of income for a composer. The pleasant atmosphere is conducive to creativity, and the availability of musicians to play the compositions is a great asset. For example, John Corigliano, Composer and Distinguished Professor, Lehman College, has been teaching composition and orchestration there for more than two decades. Professor Corigliano has composed a huge and notable body of work, including a commission from the Metropolitan Opera Company in New York City to compose the opera *Ghosts of Versailles*, which had its debut at the Met in 1992. He is also the recipient of the Pulitzer prize for his *Second Symphony for String Orchestra* (2001), the Academy Award for his score for the film

The Red Violin (2000), and many Grammy Awards for recordings of his works.

A composer can also earn a living by teaching privately; by arranging music for shows, singers, and acts; or by working as an accompanist, conductor, choir director, vocal coach, or church musician.

The Computer Age

The computer has become an important tool for the composer. In fact, in some areas of music it has taken over completely. A computer and several synthesizers can imitate the sound of an entire orchestra, with the added advantage that electronic sounds have, an infinite range of colors. This new technology has revolutionized the music industry. A composer must be familiar with the techniques and equipment used to create these new sounds.

New England Digital (NED) created an instrument called the Synclavier. It is a highly sophisticated computer/sequencer/synthesizer/sampler and digital recorder. It has become an important tool in postproduction work for film and television. It is also used to create a music sound track without the use of live musicians.

Kurzweil, and synthesis pioneer Robert Moog, developed an instrument called the Kurzweil. It is a keyboard/sampler that can duplicate the sound of strings, horns, piano, bass, drums, and many other instruments and sounds.

Other companies such as Yamaha, Roland, AKAI, Emulater, and Korg have also created instruments that can produce thousands of sounds at the touch of a finger. Many of these synthesizer manufacturers, computer companies, and software companies employ musicians and composers with computer backgrounds for research and development, sales and promotion, and education and demonstration.

Many composers have put together what is called a MIDI (Musical Instrument Digital Interface) studio in their homes. Some use it as a composer's workstation, programming the score and sounds onto a floppy disk, and recording it as a demo. At a later date, they bring the disk to a full-blown studio to record the master. Again, all this is managed without the use of any live musicians. However, many composers and producers mix the sound of live musicians with their electronic sounds. It's all a question of budget and creative preferences. Presently the trend in Hollywood is to go back to using live musicians and large orchestras for feature films.

Some composers invest a great deal of money in their workstations and create a multitrack home studio capable of producing a broadcast-quality finished product. A home studio can cost anywhere from $10,000 to $150,000. (In the past a Synclavier alone cost from $75,000 to $500,000, and you still needed a mixing console, a multitrack recording deck, and a lot of other equipment. However, due to new technology and competition, a Synclavier can now be purchased for $15,000 to $100,000.) Digidesign has created "Pro-Tools," which uses the same digital hard-disc technology to record music and sound, and it, too, has become an important tool for postproduction in film and television. In fact, there is equipment available now that can produce broadcast-quality music in your home studio for as little as $5,000. A composer has to be willing to invest a lot of money into this type of equipment.

More important than money is time. The computer, the program, the synthesizer, the sampler, the mixing console, the recording deck, and all the other pieces of equipment that go into a studio have to be studied, for each has its own technology. And, although these high-tech instruments can create great sounds and interesting sequences, it still takes a composer to turn these sounds and sequences into a musical composition.

Many composers use computer programs to score film and television. Two popular programs are: "Performer" by Mark of the Unicorn (MOTU), motu.com, and "Film Composers Time Processor" by Auricle Control Systems, webcom.com/~auricle.

There are rewards for those who succeed. A musician who is skilled in computer/synthesis technology (sometimes referred to as a programmer) can earn anywhere from minimum wage to several thousand dollars per week, depending on his or her stature in the industry and the project and/or artist with whom he or she works.

Many local schools have courses, workshops, and seminars in this new technology. For example, there is The New School University (New York City), nsu.newschool.edu; The Guitar Study Center (New York City), nsu.newschool.edu; Harvestworks Digital Media Arts Center (New York City), harvestworks.org; and the Indiana University Center for Electronic and Computer Music, www.indiana.edu/~emusic. The local music dealer who sells this type of equipment can be another good source of information.

For books on this subject, check *Mix Magazine*, mixmag.com; Alexander Books, abooks.com; *Keyboard Magazine*, keyboard mag.com; and *Electronic Musician*, emusician.com.

The Arranger/Orchestrator

A composer creates the theme and melody, the harmony, and the countermelody (counterpoint). An arranger adapts and prepares this already written melody and harmony for a performance, with a beginning (intro), middle, repeats, modulations, variations, and an ending. The orchestrator scores the arrangement, dividing the voices and assigning them to various instruments.

An orchestrator must know the range of instruments and how to blend them for specific sounds and effects. In some instances the composer, arranger, and orchestrator can be the same person. Most times, however, the work is contracted out to two or three different people.

In film scoring, a composer is hired to write the main theme and underscore. A lyricist will be hired if the producer wants words set to the main theme. In some films, songwriting teams are hired, in addition to the composer, to create specific songs for the film. An arranger and/or the composer then synchronizes the music to match the film's hit points (specific points of action); they arrange each music cue to fit its specific mood and duration in time. This is all calculated from the timing sheets (a feet and frame readout of the film supplied by the music editor). The tempo is then translated into a click track, a special metronome used for film scoring. An orchestrator is called in to score the composition for each music cue, a copyist copies the music from the score and notates it onto individual charts (music paper) for each instrument. Then an orchestra and a conductor go into a recording studio, called a scoring stage. And, finally, through this combination of artistry and technology, the movie comes alive with music.

Film and Television

Major studios, producers, and networks have a music director. The person who holds this executive position usually has a music background and comes from the A&R (artist & repertoire) department of a record company. The music director oversees all the music business and production for the company. Generally speaking, he or she does not have creative input, but the music director is familiar with artists, composers, and songwriters, and sometimes is called upon for an expert opinion.

Music Supervisor

"Music supervisor" is a fairly recent title in the film industry; it started in the early 1980s. Supervisors are similar to the music director, except that music supervisors do have creative input. In most cases this is a freelance position, and music supervisors generally work on one specific film project. They are responsible for setting up budgets and schedules and negotiating with composers, lyricists, songwriters, and artists. Music supervisors act as liaison between the producer, director, composer, publisher, record company, film editor, and music editor. Their duties include handling all the paperwork with regard to copyrights, licensing, reuse fees, and the sound track deal. Music supervisors help select songs, as well as coordinate and sometimes produce the music.

Music Editor

Another important position is that of music editor. This person works very closely with the composer. Music editors are usually film editors who may or may not have a background in music, but have a good feel for and understanding of music. Along with the director, producer, film editor, and composer, music editors attend the spotting session to determine where the music will be placed in the film. Music editors take notes regarding the music cues; they prepare timing sheets and click tracks for the composer. They are like a silent partner in the whole process.

If the final cut is on video, then a SMPTE time code (hours-minutes-seconds-frames) is "burned" into the picture and onto one of the audiotracks, for use as a reference guide. Sometimes music editors are called upon to prepare a "temp track"—a temporary music track made from already existing songs and music cues that are similar to the final music. Temp tracks serve as a working guide for editors and directors, as well as a model for the composer.

Music editors belong to the Motion Picture and Videotape Editors Guild, 7715 Sunset Boulevard, Hollywood, CA 90046; www.editorsguild.com.

A good guide to motion picture and TV development and production companies is the *Hollywood Creative Directory*, www.hcd online.com, hollywoodreporter.com, and variety.com.

Production Music Libraries

Approximately twenty-five to thirty production companies produce music that is not "original," that is, not written for a specific project. The type of music they publish is also referred to as library music or stock music, and it came into existence in 1927.

Some companies have composers on staff, and others hire them on a freelance basis. Freelance composers are sometimes paid for the composition up front, or they work on speculation. Use of the music is called a "needle drop" or "drop," and the user must pay a fee, which is split evenly by the production company and the composer. If the music is broadcast on TV or radio, it then generates an ASCAP, BMI, or SESAC royalty. Composers can earn up to

$100,000 or more per year depending on if, and how, their music is used.

The music is written according to certain specifications, such as romantic moods, chase music, fanfares, dream sequences, and so on. Sometimes the music is composed to specific lengths, like fifteen seconds or five minutes. The music is written for small combos on up to symphony orchestras, and it covers all styles, such as jazz, country, and pop. The music is used by audiovisual companies, industrial producers, schools, broadcasters, as well as film and TV producers.

Background Music

There are three major companies that supply what is called "background music," sometimes referred to as "wallpaper music." You've experienced it many times—in a doctor's waiting room, in an elevator, in a restaurant, and in the workplace. It is broadcast via satellite to a location, or purchased as an on-location service, with the music company supplying a CD player or tape deck and special cassettes and CDs.

These companies sometimes license original works from composers; however, the piece must be recorded in a professional studio using acoustic instruments. Homemade MIDI/synthesizer recordings are not accepted. The background music company generally hires a production company to record songs for their catalog of standard and contemporary songs. The production company then hires the orchestrator, the arranger, the musicians, and the recording studio. Vocalists are never used.

As part of their service, the background music company pays the licensing fee to ASCAP, BMI, and SESAC, who in turn pay the composers a royalty for the use of their music. Approximately eight producers, in about five or six cities, produce this type of music. Their catalog includes small combos as well as large orchestras, and the style of music is categorized as contemporary classic, new age, light jazz, soft rock, and adult contemporary.

Breaking into the Industry

If you want to be a composer, try to get a job with a producer of background music or demonstration records, or anything that will give you the opportunity to be around composers and orchestrators. Do copy work or menial office chores, even sweep the floors. You may hear of a new producer looking for an arranger or an orchestrator, or there may be some overflow work you can handle. If you are not in the office, or the studio, they'll never know you, and you'll never know them. Many composers get their break by orchestrating for established composers. If you're working in a studio or have a home studio, record some samples of your own themes and orchestrations; then use the tape or CD as a demo to show your talents. Keep it short.

There are also opportunities to gain experience as a volunteer. Producers of public affairs commercials always need talented and eager composers who are willing to donate their time and expertise. Look in the trade papers, like *Backstage*, *Variety*, and the *Hollywood Reporter*.

Student film projects quite often need music, and working for a student director will give you a sample of your work. Also, you will be meeting the future producers and directors who will one day be creating major feature films and television. For example, Dr. Ron Sadoff, director of the film music studies program at New

York University's Steinhardt School of Education, gives his students the opportunity to compose original music for short films and animations for the graduate students at the Tisch School of the Arts, Maurice Kanbar Institute of Film and Television. This collaboration is regularly presented as a live performance in the Film Society of Lincoln Center's "Golden Silents" series.

In the month of June, NYU and ASCAP sponsor the Buddy Baker[1] Film Scoring Workshop, where students are given a clip of a feature film, taught the techniques of scoring, and then compose and orchestrate their music for an orchestra comprised of professional musicians as well as members of the New York Philharmonic. This is done with the cooperation of Local 802, AFofM[2].

The music cues are recorded and mixed "with picture," then screened and critiqued. Along with the learning and networking processes, each member of the workshop then has a video and audio sample of his or her work. Check with a college or university film department, media department, or communications department near you for opportunities.

In addition, studying with a composer or an arranger can give you many tips on finding work. Belonging to the Musicians Union and to other professional organizations should also get you some leads. Once you've got your first assignment, you will have a sample of your work and the proof of your worth.

Film director Steven Stockage, while giving a lecture entitled "The Language of Film," recommended to the composers wishing

---

1. Buddy Baker, a "Disney Legend," is the program director of Scoring for Motion Pictures and Television at the University of Southern California. Dr. Baker served as the Composer/Musical Director for Walt Disney for twenty-eight years and has scored dozens of movies.

2. The musicians' union in New York City.

to do film music that they should be involved with organizations like The Independent Feature Project and The New York Women in Film and Television, whose membership is made up of aspiring film and video directors and producers. These organizations host events and seminars that not only educate and inform the membership about the business and techniques of the industry, but they also offer the film/video maker and the composer a forum in which to network. Contact these and other industry organizations at:

Film Music Network and *Film Music Magazine*
Film Music Media Group
150 South Glenoaks Bouldevard, Suite 600
Burbank, CA 91502
filmmusicworld.com

Film Score Magazine
8503 Washington Boulevard
Culver City, CA 90232
filmscoremonthly.com

Filmmaker Magazine
filmmakermagazine.com

The Independent Feature Project
104 West Nineteenth Street
New York, NY 10001
ifp.org
(The IFP has locales in California, Illinois, Florida, and Minnesota.)

New York Women in Film and Television
6 East Thirty-ninth Street
New York, NY 10016-0112

nywift.org
(NYWIFT has chapters and affiliates in this country and around the world.)

The Society of Composers and Lyricists
400 South Beverly Drive, Suite 214
Beverly Hills, CA 90212
filmscore.org

youngcomposers.com

The Copyist

Copyists freelance or work for a copy service or a publishing company. A knowledge of music, transposition, and music notation is necessary. Since copying is the drawing of notes on the staff (or staves), it requires good penmanship. If you enjoy this type of work, you might consider working for a publisher. Copyists, transcribers, and autographers are all needed to prepare sheet music for printers. There are also computer programs capable of printing music. Music copyists should also familiarize themselves with these computer techniques.

Some popular computer notation programs include Finale (codamusic.com), Mosaic (motu.com), Sibelius (www.sibelius.com), and Autoscore (dw.com.au/autoscore).

Pay scales for copy work are per-page and per-hour, depending on the nature of the work. The AFM (American Federation of Musicians) Phonograph Record Labor Agreement publishes the following scales:

> Composing and arranging are considered creative skills; therefore, the fees are left to the individuals doing the work. However, an

arranger's fee cannot be less than the orchestrator's fee. Where the arranger is also the orchestrator, he or she will receive the orchestration fee in addition to the arranging fee.

According to AFM's 2001 list, the hourly rate for an orchestrator was $40.73; this varies according to the size of the orchestra, style of music, and stature of the orchestrator. The hourly rate for a copyist was $21.01, and the page rate varied according to the part. All rates are variable according to style and specifications of the music. Orchestrating and copying for television, theater, and feature film each have different pay rates.

You must have samples of your work to present to music houses, producers, composers, orchestrators, arrangers, sheet music publishers, songwriters, singers, and anyone else who might need your services.

Advertising Music

Writing advertising music is an art and trade in itself. Most advertising music is produced in New York; Los Angeles and Chicago also have a good share of the business. However, there are other jingle producers all over the country.

A music production company, sometimes called a music house, is usually responsible for the jingle and the scoring. Most music houses are self-contained; the owners are the composers, songwriters, instrumentalists, singers, producers, arrangers, and contractors. The copy work is sometimes done by someone else; however, music houses tend to use the same people over and over again.

Some music production companies maintain their own recording studio and compose and produce everything in-house. A job with a music house can give you the opportunity to be in the right place at the right time. If you can get some of the overflow to write, or get to perform on the demos, you can build a reputation for yourself and collect samples of your work. If you play an instrument or sing, working on the bread-and-butter jobs can give you leads and sustain you as you make your rounds with your presentation reel.

A good source of information on commercial production and advertising industry news is *Shoot Magazine*, 770 Broadway, New York, NY 10003.

From Concept to Airplay

An advertising agency creative director (CD) gets an assignment to create a concept for a new client's product. The CD then assigns the project to one or more creative teams under his or her supervision. The teams consist of an art director and a copywriter. Each team comes up with several ideas for radio and television commercials, and they all need music.

All the concepts for the ad campaign are presented, and the best idea is then selected. At that point a producer is brought in to coordinate the entire production of the spots. The producer may be someone on staff or a freelance person. The producer, creative director, art director, and copywriter (who is also the lyricist) decide what type of music and which composer to use. They then call on their music director—if the agency is large enough to have one—to help with their decision. The music director, or the producer, has a file of composer's tapes, from which they select the style they like best.

Next, they call in several composers to create a demo and a budget. There is usually a small fee for this service. The composers use either the storyboard or the video as a guide. In most cases the composers must present their ideas the next day, and, of course, the best one is selected.

Musicians are multitalented, and many of today's jingle writers have worked as advertising copywriters, producers, or art directors. A job with an advertising agency or a music house can open many doors for an aspiring jingle writer. However, with today's technology more and more commercials are made by composers who are also sound designers and have the technology to sample and create sounds that can be organized into a rhythmic or melodic pattern.

Good sources of information on the advertising industry are: the *Film and Television Directory* and *Fashion and Print Directory* (both available from Peter Glenn Publications, 49 Riverside Avenue, Westport, CT 06880, pgdirect.com), and the *Backstage TV Film & Tape Production Directory* (Backstage Publications, New York). Each lists advertising agencies, film producers, TV producers, and music houses.

Industrials

An industrial is a film, video, musical theater piece, or musical revue that advertises a product or a company. It could be a series of songs about a corporation, a state, a car, or a beverage. Very often composers, arrangers, and copyists are used to write and produce the original music. *Screen and Stage Directory* (Peter Glenn Publications, pgdirect.com) publishes a list of industrial producers.

Musical Theater

In the 1920s through the 1940s, Broadway—The Great White Way—played host to composers like George M. Cohan, Cole Porter, George Gershwin, Jerome Kern, and Irving Berlin. These composers left a legacy of songs that are part of America's everyday life, songs that are still played and sung all over the world. There's no excitement like a Broadway show, the thrill of opening night, and the applause that's heard around the world if the show is a hit.

Songs for Broadway musical theater are created through the collaboration of a composer and a lyricist. An arranger expands the songs into dance numbers, chorus numbers, overtures, reprises, and whatever else is needed. The music is then orchestrated and copied. Finally, after many months of rehearsal, a conductor directs the pit musicians and the stage actors through an opening night performance that will either make or break the show.

Because of the tremendous production costs involved in creating a Broadway show, few producers are willing to take a chance on young, unproven composers. So, for new composers, Off-Off Broadway, Off-Broadway, showcases, revues, and regional theaters are the best venues for getting attention. Many hit musicals are now getting their start in regional theater and in Europe.

Creating a Show

How would you create a Broadway show? Find a book, a lyricist, and a playwright, and just start composing the songs. When you've finished, get financial backers. To do this, put together a backers' audition tape, which is a demonstration tape with all the songs in sequence. Gather a group of potential backers to listen to you, with your tape player running. You and your partners, or professional actors, narrate the story line, or read the lines from the script, and play the songs as needed. If the backers and the producer like it, you are on your way to becoming a musical theater composer.

How do you find a lyricist? By working in and around the Broadway scene! Working for a producer, or even a literary agent, can afford you the opportunity to meet theater people. Actors often write plays; perhaps that's a way to find a good story to convert into a musical.

Organizations to Contact

Organizations such as the Songwriters Guild of America, ASCAP, BMI, and the Dramatists Guild have seminars for composers and lyricists of the musical theater. The NEA awards grants for special theater projects, and there are many organizations that help and encourage new writers.

The Dramatists Guild of America, Inc. (1501 Broadway, Suite 701, New York, NY 10036, dramaguild.com) is a professional organization whose membership consists of playwrights, lyricists, and composers. The guild sponsors workshops and symposia across the country, in which experienced professionals discuss various aspects of writing for the theater. The guild has a special contract form that members can use in drawing up contracts between themselves and producers. In addition, the guild publishes the *Dramatists Guild Quarterly* and a newsletter.

The Songwriter

The song is where it all begins; without a song there would be no singer, no musician, and thus no music business. There are approximately three thousand music publishers listed in Billboard's *International Buyers Guide*, and every one of them has songwriters knocking on their door.

It all began in turn-of-the-century New York City, on a street called Tin Pan Alley. Songwriters went from publisher to publisher with their songs, hoping that one of them would sell and become a hit. It's no different today. From New York to Nashville to Los Angeles, wherever a publisher sets up shop, newcomers try to sell their songs. The styles may change, the song forms may change, but the demand for good music never ceases.

Making Contacts

There are several good ways for songwriters to make contacts. Songwriting clubs exist all around the country. Their members all share the same interest in writing a song that gets published and recorded, becomes a hit, and makes its author rich and famous. In some areas there are nightclubs that showcase songwriters. Check the yellow pages or ask musicians at local clubs. You can also get information from the music department of the college or university in your area. The trade papers, like *Billboard*, are very good sources of information. If you get frustrated, make a long distance call to one of them. Someone will help you.

If you are serious about songwriting, you should belong to several songwriters' organizations in order to make contacts, find collaborators, and get information. Groups like the Songwriters Guild of America (SGA), Nashville Songwriters Association International (NSAI), American Society of Composers, Authors and Publishers (ASCAP), Broadcast Music Inc. (BMI), and the National Academy of Popular Music (NAPM) [also known as the Songwriters Hall of Fame] are good choices. They all have pamphlets and booklets to help you learn the business of songwriting. They also have seminars and workshops to help you network and learn the craft of songwriting.

Financial Arrangements

Songwriters freelance or work on staff with publishers. Some songwriters are signed to one publisher, and everything they write belongs to that company. Others are on a first-refusal basis, which means the publisher has the option of buying or refusing a song. If the publisher refuses to buy it, then the songwriter is free to sell to another publisher.

A publisher buys a song by signing a contract, usually giving the songwriter a small advance, and agreeing to pay royalties. Staff writers are paid a small salary that is considered an advance on their royalties. Royalties are fees based on record sales, sheet music sales, airplay, and public performances.

Organizations like ASCAP, BMI, and SESAC collect fees from radio and TV broadcasters, restaurants, clubs, hotels, and whoever else uses music for profit. Each group has its own special surveys and complicated formulas for determining fees, which are divided proportionately according to the rate at which each composition is played. The royalty is divided into two parts paid directly by the licensing agency. Part of the royalty goes to the publisher and the other goes to the writer or writers.

Organizations like the Harry Fox Agency collect mechanical royalties from record companies. A mechanical is a phonograph record, cassette tape, or a compact disk (CD). Under the old copyright law, the royalty rate was two cents per song. This royalty would be collected by the Harry Fox Agency and distributed accordingly. The 1976 Copyright Act created the Copyright Royalty Tribunal (CRT), which was made up of five commissioners appointed by the President. The CRT met every two years to adjust the mechanical royalty rate. However, the Copyright Royalty Tribunal is no longer in existence, and the rates are now set by the Copyright Arbitration Royalty Panel, which was established in 1993. The mechanical rate from January 1, 2001 to December 31, 2001 is 7.55 cents, or 1.45 cents per minute of playing or fraction thereof, whichever is greater.

A song has to sell a lot of cassettes, CDs, or sheet music and get a large amount of radio and TV exposure in order for a writer to make a substantial amount of money. Even if a song is a hit, it takes a long time for the money to filter down through the system into the writer's pocket. At one time, licensing agencies (such as ASCAP and BMI) gave advances to publishers and songwriters, but because of legal difficulties, the practice of giving advances has been discontinued, except in cases of extreme hardship. And, according to the National Music Publishers Association, home taping currently accounts for more than a billion dollars in annual losses to the music industry internationally.

Where to Start

The three main music centers for songwriters are New York, Nashville, and Los Angeles. Some other markets are Toronto, Shreveport, Muscle Shoals, Chicago, Miami, Minneapolis, Atlanta, and Boston. However, before you move to a music center, be sure you have a job waiting for you or enough money saved to sustain yourself during your quest. Songwriters face stiff competition today. Many recording and publishing companies use artists who write their own material, which leaves very little room for outside writers. If you sing or play an instrument, you might be able to get a job as an entertainer, but remember that many other songwriters will have the same idea.

Since there are more than enough songwriters showcasing their talents and seeking recognition, the likelihood of being paid for your talent is slim. You could end up pumping gas, waiting tables, or even going home broke and disillusioned. A better way to start might be to work in your hometown, using the phone and mail to make some contacts with publishers. Then make a few visits to build your contacts. Once you've saved enough money to support yourself and have built some solid contacts, then consider relocating.

A songwriter needs instruments, reference materials, recording equipment, a computer, lead sheets (sheet music), copyrights, and demos—all of which are expensive. Phone calls, postage, stationery, and lunch dates can also be very costly.

Close association with other songwriters, publishers, artists, and producers is also essential for a songwriter to gain recognition. A songwriter must do homework to learn what type of music each publisher handles, who the professional manager is, what style of songs is selling, and which artists, producers, and record labels use outside material. An excellent guide for a songwriter, *Songwriters Market*, is published yearly by F & W Publications, Inc., 1507 Dana Avenue, Cincinnati, OH 45207, writersdigest.com.

A good way to get exposure for yourself and your songs is through songwriter showcases and contests. The following would be a good start. For application, rules, and deadline dates write:

The Billboard Song Contest
P.O. Box 470306
Tulsa, OK 74147-0306
billboard.com/billboard/songcontest/index.jsp

The John Lennon Songwriting Contest
83 Riverside Drive
New York, NY 10024
jlsc.com

Copyrights

To show ownership of a piece of music, you simply have to affix the copyright notice, which is a small *c* in a circle ©, the abbreviation COPR, or the word *copyright*. This information is followed by the year and the name of the copyright owner. (Example: © 2001 Bob Gerardi.) Once a composition is fixed, as a lead sheet or a recording, it is automatically copyrighted. However, to file ownership and to protect the song, you must register it with the Copyright Office in Washington, D.C.

It is not possible to copyright song ideas or titles. A lead sheet showing the melody of the work, with or without the words, can be filed with Application PA, or a tape recording of the work can be filed with Application SR. Send the application, sample of the work, and a filing fee to the Copyright Office, Library of Congress, 101 Independence Avenue SE, Washington, D.C. 20559-6000; www.loc.gov/copyright. Then the song is registered and protected. If you're a prolific writer, copyrighting each song can be expensive. It would be advisable to wait until you have a group of songs and file them as a collection.

Although filing a copyright is a simple procedure, copyright law is a very involved and complicated area. Learn as much about copyrights as possible, so that you can understand the law as it applies to you. Information, applications, and circulars are available from the Copyright Office.

Organizations Helpful to Composers and Songwriters

American Composers Alliance
73 Spring Street, Room 506
New York, NY 10012
composers.com

American Music Center
30 West Twenty-sixth Street, Suite 1001
New York, NY 10010-2011
amc.net

American Society of Composers, Authors and Publishers (ASCAP)
One Lincoln Plaza
New York, NY 10023
ascap.com

American Society of Music Arrangers and Composers
P.O. Box 17840
Encino, CA 91416
asmac.org

Broadcast Music Inc. (BMI)
320 West Fifty-seventh Street
New York, NY 10019
bmi.com

Canadian League of Composers
composition.org

The Foundation Center
79 Fifth Avenue, 8th Floor
New York, NY 10003-3076
fdncenter.org/newyork
or
312 Sutter Street, Suite 606
San Francisco, CA 94108-4323
fdncenter.org/sanfrancisco
or
1627 K Street NW
Washington, D.C. 20006-1708
fdncenter.org/washington
or
Kent H. Smith Library
1422 Euclid Avenue
Cleveland, OH 44115-2001
fdncenter.org/cleveland
or
Suite 150, Grand Lobby
50 Hurt Plaza, Suite 150
Atlanta, GA 30303-2914
800-424-9836
fdncenter.org/atlanta

Nashville Songwriters Association International (NSAI)
1701 West End Avenue, 3rd Floor
Nashville, TN 37203
www.nashvillesongwriters.com

The National Academy of Popular Music (NAPM)
330 West Fifty-eighth Street, Suite 411
New York, NY 10019
songwritershalloffame.org

National Association of Composers/USA
P.O. Box 49652
Barrington Station
Los Angeles, CA 90049
www.music-usa.org/nacusa

NEA, National Endowment of the Arts
1100 Pennsylvania Avenue NW
Washington, D.C. 20506-0001
arts.gov

SESAC
55 Music Square East
Nashville, TN 37203
sesac.com
or
501 Santa Monica Boulevard, Suite 450
Santa Monica, CA 90401-2430
or
421 West Fifty-fourth Street
New York, NY 10019

The Society of Composers and Lyricists
400 South Beverly Drive, Suite 214
Beverly Hills, CA 90212
filmscore.org

The Songwriters Guild of America (SGA)

1500 Harbor Boulevard
Weehawken, NJ 07086
songwriters.org
or
6430 Sunset Boulevard, Suite 705
Hollywood, CA 90028
or
1222 Sixteenth Avenue South, Suite 25
Nashville, TN 37212
or
1560 Broadway, Suite 1306
New York, NY 10036

4

Music Publishing

Music publishing can be categorized into three basic areas: (1) standard music publishing, which specializes in classical and serious contemporary music; (2) educational music publishing, which specializes in music instruction books and school band music; and (3) popular music publishing, which concentrates on new songs and the standard popular songs of the past that are played on the radio, TV, CDs, and in film.

Music publishing consists of presenting music for sale to the public, in print or in sound. Printed music is sheet music or a collection of songs in book form; the sale of printed music profits the publisher and provides a royalty for the writer(s). Sound publication of music is music recorded and presented to the public as a cassette tape, a CD, or in a sound track; the sale of CDs also results in a profit for the record company and a royalty to the publisher and the writer(s). CD royalties are called mechanical fees. Broadcasting music over radio or TV, using it in a film, or performing it live, obligates the user to pay a performance royalty to the publisher(s) and the writer(s).

Publishers are all over the country, but the main concentration is in the three music centers: New York, Nashville, and Los Angeles. Salaries in music publishing range from $20,000 (entry-level) to $100,000 per year or more depending on the job, the location, and the person's status in the industry.

Professional Manager

A professional manager is the person at a music publishing company who finds new material and promotes it. Depending on the size of the company, the professional manager may have many responsibilities. He or she is a combination of song promoter and talent scout. Managers may listen to songs submitted through the mail, sit with songwriters and listen to their tapes, or attend live performances in search of new material and writers. Many large publishers have staff songwriters who present their compositions to the professional manager.

The professional manager must have a good ear for music, be tuned in to the everyday business of music, listen to the radio constantly, read the trade papers, and be familiar with the popular music charts. Perhaps the most important part of the job is the ability to hear a commercial song and know which recording artist is best suited to perform it. Many of today's popular artists write their own songs, and some even have their own publishing companies. Therefore, a professional manager must know which artists will consider performing someone else's material.

The professional manager also must be familiar with the company's catalog. Many of today's pop hits were written 5, 10, or 15 years ago. New arrangements of standards that were hits years ago often become new hits of today. Warner/Chappel Music, one of the largest publishers in the world, maintains a catalog of approximately three hundred thousand titles.

After listening to the numerous submissions, the professional manager reviews selected songs at a weekly meeting of the professional staff. The songs finally selected and signed are made into demos so that each of the professional managers can "pitch" them to a special artist. Getting a song to a recording artist can be a real challenge. Each artist is associated with a manager, an agent, a producer, a record company, a publishing company, an arranger/conductor/accompanist, and a band. A professional manager has to do a great deal of planning to find a way of getting a song to a particular artist. Sometimes the demo of the song is recorded with a sound similar to that of the artist in mind. Sometimes, when several artists are being considered, several versions of the song might be recorded.

The professional manager must be creative in directing the producer of the demos toward different styles. He or she must be familiar with the recording studio, musicians, singers, arrangers, and engineers. In some cases, professional managers produce the demos themselves. A professional manager must know how to budget a demo session and which arrangers, musicians, and singers to call for the session.

The professional manager is really a salesperson, selling songs, and he or she must have a good personality and strong contacts with producers, artists, and record companies. A manager's work never ends. Once the song is recorded and released, he or she must "work" the song to get other artists to include it on their upcoming CD albums. For example, suppose the original artist sold one million CDs of the song. Meanwhile nine other artists also recorded it on their albums, and they each sold one million CDs.

The publisher and writer would then receive royalties from ten million CDs.

Transcriber

In order for the song to be made into a demo, copyrighted, and presented, a lead sheet (sheet music) must be prepared. A transcriber is hired to make the lead sheet. The transcriber may be on the staff, or work freelance. He or she listens to the recorded music and writes the notes of the melody and harmony on music paper. A transcriber (similar to a copyist) must have a good knowledge of music notation, a good ear, and a neat and artistic penmanship. Courses in dictation and ear training can prepare a person to transcribe.

Copyright Manager

Once a song is published, it must be copyrighted. This is usually done by the copyright department manager, who may also be responsible for rights and permissions. A basic knowledge of copyright law and licensing procedures is necessary to do this job. A person seeking a career in music publishing should also be familiar with the functions of the Harry Fox Agency, the American Society of Composers, Authors and Publishers (ASCAP), Broadcast Music Inc. (BMI), and SESAC.

Tape Copier

Every music publisher has a small room where the tape or CD copies are made. Sometimes a person breaking into the business is given the title of tape copier and is responsible for making the cassette tapes or CDs, which are called transfers or dubs.

More often, the professional manager makes the tape or CD copy. A basic knowledge of recording techniques is needed to make transfers. As simple as this operation may seem, it takes time and care to be sure that the copy has been properly prepared and checked before it is sent out.

Sheet Music Preparation

After a song has been recorded and begins to get airplay, the sheet music is prepared, especially if the song is on its way to becoming a hit. An arranger is hired to prepare a piano/voice and guitar arrangement of the song. In some companies the arranger is on staff, otherwise a freelance arranger may be hired.

After the arrangement is completed, it is passed on to an editor who checks it for errors in notation and spelling. The editor must have a good knowledge of music notation, harmony, and theory and an understanding of the style of music he or she is working on. In the case of band and orchestra arrangements, the editor must be familiar with orchestration, transposition, and the ranges of instruments.

In the past the manuscript was given to the engraver, who carved the music notes onto a plate. Today a typographer types the music notes with a special typewriter or computer. An autographer uses a special pen to write the music by hand. When the sheet music is completed, a proofreader checks the music against the original manuscript, and sometimes the composer also proofs the music.

An artist designs the cover—coordinating color, photographs, and design. Finally, the printer manufactures the finished sheet music, which is then distributed to music stores and made available to the public.

Advertising

The popularity of the CD is what advertises a song; as sales go up, so do sheet music sales. In the cases of concert music, educational music, and classical music, however, it takes planned advertising to gain public attention. An advertising specialist, together with a copywriter and layout artist, plans the campaign. Salespeople, lecturers, and clinicians bring the music into the field, show it, explain it, and demonstrate it. Everyone involved in the campaign must have a love and knowledge of music in order to properly represent it.

Getting into Publishing

According to Isidro Otis, President, Clyde Otis Music Group, industry executives are always looking for bright, young, talented people who are eager to learn. Although a person may know and love music and be a musician and a songwriter, there are some other basic skills that can open the door to a career in music publishing.

The ability to type is very important. Copyright forms, letters, lyric sheets, contracts, and envelopes all require typing. Knowing how to type, operate a tape recorder, and work on a computer can play an important part in getting you that first job.

People in publishing are self-motivated and, in most cases, learn their trade on the job. A good source of information is the Music and Entertainment Industry Educators Association (MEIEA). For information go to meiea.org. The following resources will also be helpful for those interested in music publishing.

Trade Publication

Billboard

770 Broadway, 6th Floor
New York, NY 10003
billboard.com

Trade Organizations

Association of Independent Music Publishers

120 East Fifty-sixth Street
New York, NY 10022
aimp.org
or
P.O. Box 1561
Burbank, CA 91507-1561

Harry Fox Agency

7111 Third Avenue
New York, NY 10017
nmpa.org

Music Publishers' Association of the United States

1562 First Avenue
New York, NY 10028
mpa.org

National Music Publishers' Association
475 Park Avenue South, 29th Floor
New York, NY 10016-6901
nmpa.org

5

Professional Organizations

Professional organizations give musicians, singers, and writers opportunities to meet and network with people who share common interests. These organizations help make the public aware of the needs of their members. They establish codes of ethics, working conditions, and standards of excellence. They franchise agents and negotiate wages, health, and pension benefits with employers. Many professional organizations maintain pension plans, health plans, and credit unions, and most keep members informed through their many publications. Professional organizations often offer grants, scholarships, and seminars to further educate and inform their members. They also work to protect artists' rights by representing them in Washington, D.C.

For example, in the mid 1990s the National Endowment for the Arts was under attack for funding controversial artwork. Of the 75,000 grants awarded in the NEA's twenty-five year history, only two dozen have sparked public debate. Yet critics targeted the NEA for extinction. Since this would have been a devastating loss to the arts community, professional organizations informed their membership and encouraged them to write to their congressional representatives and senators in support of the NEA.

Other problems are the DAT (digital audiotape) recorders and downloading music on the Internet. As mentioned before, billions of dollars in royalties are lost to analog home tape recording. A DAT recorder and CD burner makes it possible to record perfect, distortion-free, first-generation copies of CDs, digital broadcasts, and downloads, which would encourage even more people to make their own tapes at home, resulting in even more lost royalties for music creators. The National Music Publishers' Association (NMPA), the Songwriters Guild of America (SGA), and the American Society of Composers, Authors and Publishers (ASCAP) formed the Copyright Coalition. The Coalition filed a class action suit charging that DAT recorders and blank DAT cassettes interfere with federal copyrights. The Coalition also created a copying safeguard known as the Serial Copying Management System (SCMS). They successfully lobbied for the home-taping royalty bill, which went into effect in 1992. It attaches a surcharge to the hardware and blank tapes that is then passed on to the music creators.

American Federation of Musicians of the United States and Canada (AFM)

The American Federation of Musicians of the United States and Canada was founded in 1896. It is one of the oldest of the performance unions. The AFM (1501 Broadway, New York, NY 10036, afm.org) has approximately 110,000 members in more than 250 locals throughout the United States and Canada. Members are instrumentalists, arrangers, orchestrators, copyists, proofreaders, conductors, librarians, and vocalists.

The AFM represents musicians in phonograph, film, TV, and commercial recordings; radio and TV broadcasting; the concert field; musical theater; opera; ballet; ice shows; the circus; and in steady engagements and single engagements. The AFM and its locals set working conditions within their jurisdictions for minimum size of orchestra, wage scales, special fees for doubling, travel, overtime, and rehearsal fees.

Members pay their local an initiation fee plus yearly dues and small work dues from each job. The local, in turn, pays the AFM dues on behalf of the member. The AFM has its own contract forms both for steady and single engagements and represents the musician in cases of nonpayment. The AFM also franchises agents who must adhere to AFM rules and regulations regarding bookings, wages, and commissions.

There are restrictions for switching locals, so be sure of each local's regulations before you move. The AFM local near you should be listed in the phone book. However, if you write or call the AFM headquarters in New York, they will be happy to give you any information you need.

The official journal of the AFM is *International Musician*. It is also available to nonmembers. It contains important news items, employment opportunities, and general information for the musician. In addition, each local publishes its own newsletter.

Actor's Equity Association (AEA)

The Actor's Equity Association (165 West Forty-sixth Street, New York, NY 10036, actorsequity.org) is a union of actors who work in the theater. Singing actors who work in a musical production usually belong to AEA. Equity negotiates with the producers of Broadway, Off-Broadway, regional (LORT), summer, and dinner theaters, for working conditions, benefits, and wages. Equity also franchises agents and has its own contract form.

American Federation of Television and Radio Artists (AFTRA)

AFTRA (260 Madison Avenue, New York, NY 10016, aftra.org) is a labor union whose membership is made up of performers, actors, announcers, newscasters, sportscasters, and singers who record on video and audiotape or work live in radio and television broadcasting.

AFTRA negotiates with record companies, television and radio networks, jingle producers, and television producers for working conditions, benefits, and wage scales. AFTRA also franchises agents and publishes its own contract form.

American Guild of Musical Artists (AGMA)

AGMA (1727 Broadway, New York, NY 10019, or visit musical artists.org) represents singers and dancers who work as soloists and in chorus for the opera and the ballet, as well as soloists in the concert field.

American Guild of Variety Artists (AGVA)

AGVA (184 Fifth Avenue, New York, NY 10010, agva.org) represents performers who work in nightclubs, cabarets, resorts, circuses, and in Las Vegas hotel floor shows. A nightclub singer would belong to this union.

Screen Actors Guild (SAG)

The Screen Actors Guild (5757 Wilshire Boulevard, Los Angeles, CA 90036, sag.org) is primarily a film actors' union. However, singers and instrumentalists performing in film (on- or off-camera) also belong to SAG.

SAG negotiates with television and theatrical movie producers for working conditions, benefits, and wages. The guild also franchises agents and publishes its own contract forms.

SAG has offices in Hollywood; New York; Boston; Chicago; Detroit; Dallas; Colorado; Washington, D.C.; San Francisco; Philadelphia; San Diego; Atlanta; Phoenix; Nashville; Houston; Miami; and Hawaii.

The Songwriters Guild of America (SGA)

Founded as the Songwriters Protective Association, later changed to American Guild of Authors and Composers (AGAC), and yet again changed to Songwriters Guild, it is today known as the Songwriters Guild of America (SGA). The original name of this organization indicates its function, then and now. However, the guild not only protects, but also represents and educates songwriters. Its more than five thousand members are composers and lyricists of both serious music and popular music.

The guild publishes a recommended publishing contract that may or may not be used by its members. However, many publishers accept and use this contract form. The guild also represents songwriters in Washington, D.C., and it has been instrumental in convincing Congress that the songwriter has valid needs in terms of legislation and copyright.

The guild audits the books of publishing companies and in the past has recovered millions of dollars in royalties for its songwriter members. The Songwriters Guild of America sponsors seminars that teach the craft and business of songwriting, lyric writing, and jingle writing. It conducts an ASKAPRO session in which members (and nonmembers, for a fee) can listen and ask questions of industry professionals. There is also a song critique session where writers can get professional criticism of their materials.

The organization's newsletter, published four times a year and available to nonmembers, contains much important songwriting news. There is also a collaborator's list available. Its website is songwriters.org.

Guild offices are located in:

The Songwriters Guild of America
1500 Harbor Boulevard
Weehawken, NJ 07086
or
6430 Sunset Boulevard, Suite 705
Hollywood, CA 90028
or
1222 Sixteenth Avenue South, Suite 25
Nashville, TN 37212
or
1560 Broadway, Suite 1306
New York, NY 10036

Nashville Songwriters Association, International (NSAI)

The Nashville Songwriters Association, International (1701 West End Avenue, 3rd Floor, Nashville, TN 37203, or you can visit nashvillesongwriters.com) has a membership of more than twenty-four hundred songwriters. It has approximately eighteen workshops across the United States that have regular meetings where songwriters can discuss their craft and the business of songwriting, and critique each other's work. The association is open to songwriters in all categories of music.

The headquarters is in Nashville. NSAI maintains a list of publishers in the Nashville area. A spring symposium, open to both members and nonmembers, is held each year in Nashville. NSAI publishes a newsletter four times a year.

National Academy of Television Arts and Sciences (NATAS)

The members of NATAS represent all the crafts that produce television programming. They also present the annual Emmy Awards, locally and nationally. There are eighteen chapters nationally. The New York chapter (New York Television Academy) publishes a directory listing all its members by category. There is a music section that lists composer, arranger, conductor, instrumentalist, lyricist, music executive, music supervisor, and music producer members. For information, look them up at emmyonline.org.

Performing Rights Societies (ASCAP, BMI, SESAC)

ASCAP, BMI, and SESAC grant licenses to television and radio stations, television and radio networks, hotels, restaurants, clubs, and other users of music. A blanket license allows the user of music to publicly perform any of the copyrighted music in that society's catalog. The user pays the society a fee, which in turn is paid to the publisher and writer members whose music is being used.

American Society of Composers, Authors and Publishers (ASCAP)

The ASCAP Foundation (One Lincoln Plaza, New York, NY 10023, ascap.com) sponsors a series of workshops in New York, Nashville, and Los Angeles. The workshops are for all categories of music (film score, theater, and pop), and they are open to both ASCAP members and nonmembers. ASCAP also gives grants to young composers, as well as scholarships and awards. Major ASCAP offices are located in New York, Nashville, Los Angeles, Puerto Rico, and London, along with nineteen branch offices around the country.

Broadcast Music Inc. (BMI)

BMI (320 West Fifty-seventh Street, New York, NY 10019, www.bmi.com) awards cash prizes to composers of serious music who are under the age of twenty-six in order to help pay for their education. BMI offers a musical theater workshop in New York and sponsors a film scoring workshop in Los Angeles. BMI has offices in New York, Nashville, Los Angeles, London, Miami, Atlanta, and Puerto Rico.

SESAC

SESAC (421 West 54th Street, New York, NY 10019, sesac.com) offers its members legal advice on copyrights, placement assistance with publishers and record companies, and an artist and repertoire consultation. SESAC offices are located in New York City, Nashville, and Los Angeles.

Music Performance Trust Fund (MPTF)

The Music Performance Trust Fund is a nonprofit organization founded in 1948 as a result of an agreement between the Recording Industry of America and the American Federation of Musicians. The group was formed to offset the lack of live musical performances caused by increased use of phonograph records. Its sole purpose was, and is, to present live, admission-free, instrumental musical programs that contribute to the knowledge of and appreciation for music.

MPTF is funded by contributions from record companies based on a percentage of their sales of cassette tapes and CDs. These monies are used to present thousands of free, live programs every year throughout the United States and Canada. Businesses, schools, government agencies, banks, chambers of commerce, radio stations, hospitals, and other appropriate institutions invest additional monies as cosponsors. This helps make possible many more free, live musical events.

In one year, more than $8 million was spent to present over forty thousand live and admission-free programs in the United States and Canada in such places as veteran's hospitals, schools, block parties, nursing homes, shopping malls, and public parks. Whether a fifty-piece orchestra, large band, combo, or single strolling musician, all performances are open to the public with no charge.

A musician wishing to play an MPTF engagement should contact her or his AFM local and register with the local's MPTF Selection Committee. Payment is calculated at the local's prevailing wage, plus pension and health contributions.

6

The Popular Performer: Club Dates

Club dates (single engagements)—or casuals, as they are called in some areas—can be a good source of income for both full-time and part-time musicians and singers. Club dates are typically parties, weddings, or dinner dances, and they are usually referred to as single engagements. If you're willing to learn the necessary repertoire and perform in the style called for, then you stand a chance of making a living in the club date field.

Club date musicians generally freelance, working with different musicians on each job, forming what is called a pickup band. Suppose a bandleader books a job for an eight-piece orchestra; the first thing he or she does is hire a subleader to run the job. Then the contractor calls the rest of the musicians and books them for the job. They may have worked together before or they may be meeting for the first time on that job. The subleader calls out the tunes and tempos and coordinates and runs the job.

Some bands, on the other hand, are set units. For example, three, four, or five musicians may get together and form a group, rehearsing together to develop a repertoire and style. The trend today is to hire set groups that specialize in the current Top 40 hits of the day. Sometimes a set group is hired and then augmented with freelance club date musicians to make up a larger band and also to perform any specialized or ethnic styles of music.

The job can be in a hotel, a restaurant, a catering hall, a private home, a boat, or just about anywhere the purchaser of the music wants to have the party. This means portability, and that means equipment and transportation. You must have the equipment needed to perform (electric piano, synthesizer, amplifier, microphone, and speakers) and be able to get it to the job site. With today's instruments, that means a station wagon or a van. Jobs are often far away from your home, and you have to allow time for travel and for unloading and setting up the equipment. Some leaders hire roadies (helpers) to unload and set up.

A band is typically booked for four hours; the fifth and sixth hours are usually considered overtime. Some jobs are shorter; for instance, a fashion show or cocktail party can be one, two, or three hours. A job generally runs fifty-five minutes of playing and five minutes of break time. However, that differs from leader to leader and from area to area.

One Performer's Day

If you happen to have a club date in the afternoon, your day could last as long as sixteen hours. Suppose a wedding party starts at noon for cocktails and runs from 1:00 to 5:00 for the dinner, dancing, and ceremonies. In order to be set up by noon, you have to leave your house at 10:30, arrive at 11:30, unload and set up, and play from noon to 1:00 in the cocktail area. At 1:00 you move your equipment to the dining area and play from 1:00 to 5:00. The job is then over.

But then you have to rush to break down, load up the equipment, and drive to the next job, which starts at 7:00. You arrive at 6:30, unload, and set up. You play the cocktail party from 7:00 to 8:00, and at 8:00 you move your equipment to the dining area and make music from 8:00 to midnight. At midnight, the host of the party comes over to you and requests that you play an additional hour overtime, so you continue until 1:00 in the morning. At 1:00 you finally break down, load the car, and drive home.

As you fall into bed at 2:30 A.M., you remember that tomorrow is Sunday and you have another two engagements. That's how it goes, sometimes!

Economics

For a weekend like the one just described (four club dates), according to the 2001 Local 802 single engagement pay scale, a band member would earn more than $1,200 and the subleader would earn more than $1,800, leaving enough money for the leader to cover business expenses, taxes, pension and health contributions, and also make a profit. If the leader was very busy, the musicians could earn additional monies from some midweek work. (Saturday evening and Sunday usually pay a premium rate over the Monday through Friday scale.)

There is a lot of work in the club date field, but unfortunately there are more musicians than jobs. The constant hustle to stay employed can be very frustrating. There is also a trend to use DJs instead of live musicians, which also cuts down on the number of jobs available. However, an enterprising leader might be able to sell the client the idea of using a live band (since there is no substitute for live music) combined with a DJ for the prerecorded dance music. That way the guests will have a variety of music and entertainment.

Club dates occur all year, but there is a busy and a slow season. The busy months are May, June, October, November, and December. The other months can be very slow. Some musicians work resorts in the summer months and cruise ships in the winter months. Staying flexible and versatile is one way to survive as a freelance musician.

What It Takes to Be a Club Date Musician

Club date musicians must have not only strong backs and lots of stamina, they must also have an endless supply of songs at their fingertips. The repertoire is extremely demanding. You literally are expected to know everything, and the ability to memorize is essential. You are expected to know the music of the 1930s through current hits of today. Ethnic music, Latin American music, waltzes, specialty numbers, games, even the "Star Spangled Banner"—the club date musician plays it all.

Sight-reading is not a prerequisite for most club date bands, but it is an asset. The better bands do play for shows, and reading skills are essential. Some bands have a book (band arrangements) and, again, reading music is necessary.

In some orchestras, doubling is required—for example, guitar-bass-vocals, piano-accordion-vocals, sax-flute-clarinet, trumpetflügelhorn, violin-sax. An ability to play several instruments might get you more jobs.

You have to be able to work well with other musicians and be willing to put your ego and artistic temperament aside. Jazz virtuosity is not needed. Cooperation, attitude, and personality are all very important. Many musicians look at club dates as square music, but working them can buy a lot of square meals.

Musicianship varies from band to band. There are some very mediocre players making a good living in the club date field, but the really fine players are the ones who make the most and are always busy. A leader must have a good personality and a good sense of pacing. Most importantly, a leader must be a diplomat in order to deal with the different personalities of each client. The pressure of hosting a party sometimes causes people to act strangely. A leader must have a cool head and know how to stay calm and keep the customer smiling.

It is not necessary to belong to a union to work some club dates, but the real professionals are union members, and they play the better jobs. If you work with union professionals, you generally make contacts through them. Most musicians who work club dates freelance as studio musicians, pit musicians, nightclub performers, and so on. These are the people to know. They generally recommend musicians to each other.

Sample Repertoire

Club date musicians need to develop an extensive repertoire. Cole Porter's "Anything Goes," "From This Moment On," "I Get a Kick Out of You," or "Night and Day" are good choices. George Gershwin's "'S Wonderful," "But Not for Me," "Love Walked In," and "Nice Work if You Can Get It" are also popular. You should also know many Broadway show tunes and songs from the repertoires of other composers: Irving Berlin, Jerome Kern, Richard Rodgers, Jimmy Van Heuson, Sammy Cahn, and so on.

In addition to having a large repertoire, you should be familiar with all types of dance beats: two-beat, swing, rumba, waltz, cha-cha, rock and roll, disco, hip-hop, game dances, polka, and ethnic dances.

With all this knowledge, you will be ready for any type of club date: weddings, bar mitzvahs, birthday parties, anniversaries, graduations, dinner dances, fashion shows, retirement parties, engagement parties, beauty pageants, and Christmas parties.

Instrumental Combinations

A club date band is usually composed of musicians who play keyboard (electric piano or synthesizer), drums, sax, guitar, trumpet, and sometimes an electric bass. Because of electronic technology, electric pianos, synthesizers, and organs can simulate a bass line, so for small jobs the bass player is usually replaced by the left hand of the keyboard player.

Most trios consist of piano (acoustical), bass, and drums; or electric piano, drums, and guitar or sax.

Most quartets are made up of piano (acoustical), bass, drums, and a guitar, a sax, or a trumpet. Others combine electric piano and/or synthesizer (left hand bass), drums, guitar, and a sax or a trumpet. When more than three horns are used, make sure they can fake; otherwise, it will be necessary to have arrangements.

Big bands can include these instruments: piano, bass, drums, guitar, three trumpets, three trombones, two alto saxes, two tenor saxes, a baritone sax, and a singer(s). Any combination can be used to suit the sound of your own arrangements.

Where the Jobs Are

Restaurants, dance halls, churches, synagogues, retirement villages, prisons, condominiums, and VFW halls are all potential club date locations. All kinds of organizations hire bands: banks, corporations, labor unions, fraternal and civic groups (like Masons, Rotary Club), foundations, political parties, and hospitals.

How to Find Work

Believe it or not, if you look through the help-wanted column of the *New York Times*, you'll find an ad reading: "Musicians and singers wanted for club date work." Sometimes a local newspaper will have an advertisement for musicians and singers. Also, some band leaders advertise in the union papers.

Look in the yellow pages of your telephone book for orchestras. Or walk into a catering establishment and ask, "What's the name of the bandleader who does your work?" Find out who contracts in your area, and let him or her know that you are available for work. If you are ambitious, inventive, and persistent, you will be noticed and, eventually, you will be playing your first club date. After a while, you may become a club date leader yourself.

Studying with a professional musician who does club dates is another way of learning your way around the business. Try to meet some of the musicians who are working with your teachers, through the union, or for friends. Ask to accompany them to the jobs, help them out with their equipment, and ask questions. You'll learn. Getting into the inner circle is the key to everything. Take notes on the songs that are being played and be aware of inside tips.

Going on the Road

Although club dates are one-nighters, you don't always return home after the show. If it's very far, then you are given accommodations for the night. Working one-nighters with a band or show that travels a concert circuit is very different. A string of one-nighters can keep you on the road for months. That adds up to employment, contacts, and development of your skills.

Only the finest players are selected for road tours. Reading skills are necessary, musicianship is usually of the highest caliber, and the music can be very exciting. Some of these groups are under the baton of famous bandleaders and are put together by contractors or agents.

Steady Engagements

A steady engagement is a job that is two to six nights a week in the same place. The engagement can last for two weeks, six months, or for years. In the 1940s, large orchestras worked steady engagements in hotels and dance halls. In the 1950s, the smaller jazz and rock combos started working more steadily. Today, very few places employ large orchestras or combos for dance music. However, smaller groups and single artists are working quite a bit. There is a recent trend in some hotels to hire harpists, strolling violins, and guitarists, but the pianist is still the most popular choice.

Pianists generally work in cocktail lounges, restaurants, and hotels. Singing piano players dominate the piano bar and saloon circuit. Trio work is rare, but jobs do exist. Playing or singing in restaurants and in cocktail lounges requires a good personality, as well as good musicianship and a well-rounded repertoire. When playing in a restaurant or cocktail lounge, you can expect requests for every song ever written. Knowing the songs that are requested the most and politely bowing out when you don't know a request is important.

The better the musician, the better the job. Nightclubs, restaurants, hotels, dance halls, resorts, cruise ships, casinos, piano bars, and saloons are all possible places for steady engagements. If you're inventive, ambitious, and a good salesperson, perhaps you can create a job. In fact, there was a bank on the east side of Manhattan that featured a woman pianist who performed every day of the week.

In the early 1990s, New York City, like the rest of the country, was suffering from a recession. The hotels, clubs, and restaurants reacted to this economic decline by discontinuing their music policies and laying off many musicians. However, in the late 1990s, New York City had a major turnaround. New hotels were built, adding thousands of rooms. As tourism flourished, hotels were booked to capacity; yet despite the return of their business, they did not reinstate their music policy.

In fact, the Plaza Hotel, the icon of all hotels, recently discontinued its music policy and laid off all its musicians, including the strolling violinists and pianists in the world-famous Palm Court. The hotel still charges premium rates for its rooms, food, and drinks, but with no givebacks, in the form of entertainment, to its customers. Another example is the Marriott Marquis Hotel in midtown Manhattan, which has an automatic piano in its cocktail lounge. No live music; just premium-priced drinks.

Live music is an interactive art form; musicians and singers interact with the audience who, in turn, interacts with them through eye contact, applause, dancing, requests, and conversation. Their special talents add to the personality of the establishment. Would you sit in a concert hall and listen to prerecorded music?

Studies have shown that live music increases sales and when properly presented and promoted, it not only pays for itself but usually turns a profit. Unfortunately, nonmusic-savvy hotel managers often don't see it that way.

In a recent discussion with Bill Moriarity, the president of Local 802, AFM[1], we both agreed that music education[2] and music appreciation in schools (on all levels) is the future of "live" music. An educated consumer would and should demand live music; if these managers are exposed to quality music, and if they become aware of its aesthetic effect on the public, they will realize that live music is an elegant and profitable addition to their establishment, as well as a competitive edge.

Perhaps an enterprising musician could put together an interesting and unique proposal, using facts and figures based on statistics, to show a manager the advantages of live music, and how his or her particular brand of musical talent could benefit the hotel, restaurant, or club.

Steady work is generally rather intimate, and a lot of personal contact with the audience is necessary, so you must enjoy meeting and talking with people. Everybody loves an entertainer, and you'll

---

1. The musicians union in New York City, see Chapter 5: "Professional Organizations."

2. See Chapter 8: "Extending Career Choices," Teaching.

find yourself on a first-name basis with all the customers. That's a beginning for you, and it's how you build a following. Keep a list of the people who come into the club frequently and remember their requests. A following (or mailing list) is very important to your career.

A steady engagement can consist of middle-of-the-road music (a little bit of everything), jazz, country, Top 40 (current hits), standards, rock, Dixieland, and many other styles of music. The music can be for dancing or listening, soft and subdued, or loud and exciting. It all depends on the situation. Keeping up with current trends is very important. For instance, nostalgia is very big, and there is still a following for the big band sounds of the 1940s, the rock and roll sounds of the 1950s, and the pop sounds of the 1960s and 1970s.

Look through the entertainment section of your local paper. Make a list of all the clubs and restaurants that have live music. Make the rounds, and introduce yourself to the owners and managers.

It is not necessary to belong to the union for some of the smaller jobs, but as you upgrade your career and start working in the better rooms, you will be well served by belonging to the union. You must get work in order to gain experience and get exposure, and, of course, your second job will never happen if you don't get your first.

Pay Scale

A steady gig can pay $75 per night or it can pay $200 per night. It all depends on the club. Is it union or nonunion, small or large? Is it your first job or are you an established act? The 2001 Local

802 AFM pay scale for New York City hotel work was $750 a week (four hours a night, five nights a week) for a band member. That kind of work is nice if you can get it, but most hotel musicians stay forever, and openings are rare.

According to the same pay scale, hotels paid $938 for a solo pianist (four hours, five nights). However, a restaurant right across the street may pay less or more, depending on the act. There are many unscrupulous agents and club owners who take advantage of the overcrowded profession by paying substandard salaries.

Sometimes you get what you can according to your talent, your reputation, and the following you've achieved. A union job will also give you some benefits, such as pension, health, and vacation.

A leader or a soloist receives more money according to the size of the group. For example, a band member would receive $750; a soloist, $938; the leader of a duo, $1,125; and the leader of three or more, $1,313; plus taxes, pension, and health contributions.

These figures are based on the 2001 Local 802, AFM pay scale, four hours per night, five nights per week; different locals have different wage scales. Engagements also have different scales depending on how many hours the musicians play. (Note: A musician who doubles as a singer is entitled to an additional 15 percent premium.)

Resorts

A resort hotel is a small vacation city, and like a city it has restaurants, nightclubs, and cocktail lounges. Wherever they are, resorts have music and entertainment. Most of them have an entertainment director who works with an agent.

A simple telephone call to the music and entertainment director can provide answers to all your questions. Find out if he or she keeps files and who the agent is who books the music and entertainment. You may need to send a picture and résumé, as well as a demonstration tape and a press kit. You may get called for an audition, so have something ready.

The entertainment varies from resort to resort. Some have large bands while others have small bands. Some have full-time and others have part-time entertainment. Many resorts book name entertainers, and the band is required to play the show. That means reading skills are essential. Singer/pianist and self-contained lounge groups are used quite often.

To secure either part-time or full-time work, you have to do your homework. The pay scales vary at the resorts and usually include room and board.

Cruise Ships

Ever since the hit TV series "Love Boat" was launched, the cruise ship industry has been experiencing a boom. More and more cruises are leaving for exotic South Seas islands and around-the-world-in-eighty-days voyages. Since ships are floating resorts, it stands to reason that they have their share of restaurants, cocktail lounges, nightclubs, and piano bars. They even have small theaters. *Backstage* publishes a list of cruise ship lines, along with the agents, entertainment directors, and producers who hire the musicians, singers, dancers, and actors. One company produces small-scale versions of Broadway musicals. Another produces Las Vegas–type shows. Cruise ship musicians must be able to play dance music, play for shows, and mingle with the guests. They must have good personalities and enjoy meeting and talking with people.

Cruise ships sail from New York, Los Angeles, Florida, San Francisco, and Texas. You can find their addresses by looking through travel magazines or in the travel section of the newspaper. Call a cruise ship line and find out if it keeps its own entertainment files, if you can audition, or who the agent or producer is who books the music and entertainment.

Some musicians and entertainers are booked for long periods of time (three or six months). Some musicians make cruise work their career and stay on board for years. Salaries vary and, of course, include room and board. You are on call seven days a week and on the ship twenty-four hours a day. One big advantage of working a cruise ship is that you get to see the whole world, so if you like to travel and get paid at the same time, then the open sea may be for you.

Screen and Stage Directory (Peter Glenn Publications, pgdirect.com) has a list of cruise ship lines, agents, and producers. Here is a partial list of some cruise ship lines:

Holland America Cruises, New York
Princess Cruises, Los Angeles
Royal Viking Line, San Francisco
Scandinavian World Cruises, Miami
Cunard Lines, England
Costa Line, Miami
Easter Cruises, Miami
Paquet Lines, Miami
Carnival Cruises, Miami

Nightclub Singers

A nightclub singer is someone who sings in a nightclub and performs what is called a floor show. A singer who does a floor show, or a standup act, is either the headliner or the opening act. The opening act is sometimes referred to as a stand-up singer.

Generally, if a comedian is the star of the show, a singer is booked as the opening act. And if a singer is the star, then a comedian is the opening act. If it's a really big show, there might be a dance team, a chorus line with a production singer, or even a magic act or a mentalist.

Someone starting a career as a nightclub singer should work with a vocal coach who is familiar with the repertoire and style of nightclubs and cabarets. The singer should begin with lead sheets of the songs he or she wants to use in the act. That way songs can be tried in a showcase situation before spending money on arrangements. After enough songs have been broken in and their keys and arrangements set, they then can be transposed into piano/vocal parts or made into arrangements. To a singer, songs are like tailor-made clothes, and they must fit perfectly.

If a singer has a lot of money to spend on a show, then someone called an act builder is hired. (Sometimes the arranger will also help build the act.) The act builder creates the entire show: selection of songs, arrangements, staging, microphone technique, choreography, patter (dialogue with the audience), wardrobe, sound, and lighting. In most cases the act builder works with the pianist/accompanist, who may also be the arranger/orchestrator/conductor. Some singers work only with their own conductors, who may also play the piano while conducting the show.

Usually a singer gets a rehearsal, but since rehearsals can be expensive and time-consuming, a singer must be prepared to do a talk-over. The musicians and the leader read their charts (music) as the singer talks them through the act. A singer must be very familiar with the arrangements and know how to explain them to the musicians.

An act usually runs from thirty minutes to one hour, depending on the show. Some clubs want two different shows a night, and that could mean 8 to 17 songs per show and 16 to 34 arrangements. Some singers carry as many as 50 arrangements with them.

Although the singer's act may be set, new songs should constantly be added to keep it fresh. It's a big investment for a singer: between the act builder, choreographer, arranger, copying costs, and wardrobe, the costs could add up to thousands of dollars. Some singers have their own wireless microphones and carry their own sound systems. Before singers invest a lot of hard-earned money into an act, they should be sure they have the voice, stage presence, charisma, and personality to command center stage.

It's not easy standing on stage all alone between an orchestra and an audience. It takes a lot of energy and talent to be dynamic and exciting. A singer not only needs a good voice but must also move well. An ability to dance can be readily incorporated into the act. Many singers also have a flair for comedy, although they should be careful not to upstage any comedians who are on the bill.

A show can pay $300 or it can pay several thousand dollars; it all depends on your talent, your act, your personality, your ability to perform, and, of course, your stature in the business.

Singers work everywhere, from nightclubs to theme parks, with big bands, small bands, and in studios. The work can be seasonal and, in most cases, requires a lot of travel.

Two good sources of information for actors, singers, and dancers are the *Screen and Stage Directory* and the *Music and Sound Directory* (Peter Glenn Publications, pgdirect.com).

Theme Parks

Theme parks hire thousands of singers and musicians every season, along with actors, dancers, impressionists, and circus performers.

Rehearsals and performance schedules can be intense, but it is a great way to gain valuable experience and training. Most theme parks hire the entertainment for long periods of time—three, six, or even twelve months. Auditions are held regularly in major cities, and in some cases they are advertised in the local newspapers or in entertainment industry papers like *Backstage*.

Performances can be a solo singer with a band that lasts a few minutes, to a full-blown musical revue that lasts for an hour or more. Musical styles cover a broad range of genres and themes. Musicians are an important part of the entertainment, and they are required to read music, play different styles of music, and, in some cases, have the ability to play two instruments.

Generally the salaries are low, however, some of the specialty acts do get a higher rate of pay. Even with the low pay, the advantages are many: steady work, the experience of performing to a large audience (many times a day), developing your talents and skills, building a professional résumé, and gaining confidence in your ability to entertain. For the most part, the work is seasonal, but the larger parks run all year long.

Theme parks in the United States include the following:

Action Park, New Jersey
Busch Gardens, Virginia
Disneyland, California
Dorney Park–Wild Water Kingdom, Pennsylvania
Hershey Park, Pennsylvania
Knott's Berry Farm, California
Opryland, Tennessee
Paramount Parks, North Carolina
Silver Dollar City, Missouri
Six Flags Theme Parks, Texas
Universal Studios Florida, Florida

Walt Disney World Resort, Florida
Worlds of Fun, Missouri

You can get more information on theme parks in *Amusement Business Magazine* (amusementbusiness.com) and in the *Screen and Stage Directory* (Peter Glenn Publications, pgdirect.com).

Live Industrials

A live industrial is a theater piece or musical revue production that advertises a product or a company. For example, it could be a series of songs about a corporation, a state, a car, or a beverage. Live industrials utilize the services of singers and musicians, as well as actors and dancers. For information on industrial producers, take a look at *Screen and Stage Directory*, the *Film and Television Directory*, or the *Music and Sound Directory*, (Peter Glenn Publications, pgdirect.com).

All That Jazz

The market for jazz singers and instrumentalists is very limited. Although the musicianship is very high, the monetary rewards are very low, unless you have a hit record. Most jazz players have to play commercial music—shows, club dates, teaching, and studio work—in order to survive. American jazz is very popular in Europe and Japan, and many jazz artists travel abroad and make a living performing outside the United States.

Many jazz recording artists have combined their music with the dance rhythms of reggae, rock, disco, and Latin to get themselves onto the charts and into the concert circuit. For example, in 1970, the legendary Miles Davis won a Grammy Award for his innovative fusion album *Bitches Brew*. The album featured jazz pianist Chick Corea, who has been successful fusing jazz and Latin. Herbie Hancock's work with electronic instruments and disco dance rhythms scored him a number one hit called "Rockit." Jazz guitarist George Benson has added the sound of his singing with the sound of plush string arrangements, fusing jazz, rhythm and blues, and pop, for a successful middle-of-the-road (MOR) sound, and jazz saxophonist David Sanborn became a top-selling fusion artist.

However, classical trumpeter Wynton Marsalis, at the age of twenty-one, won two Grammys in 1983: one for Best Solo Jazz Instrumentalist and one for Best Classical Instrumentalist. He has gone on to win many more since then, as well as to score a feature film. Marsalis has begun a renaissance in jazz, and his influence has opened doors for many young players using acoustical instruments, creating a whole new market for traditional jazz. In fact the outlook for jazz is far healthier than it has been in decades.

Harry Connick, Jr., another jazz musician, started out as a jazz pianist then crossed over to the big band sound and the Sinatra style of singing that put him onto the charts and into the star category as well as into the movies.

Organizations

Many organizations offer information, money, and assistance to jazz artists. The National Endowment for the Arts has a jazz program that awards grants to jazz composers and performers. The International Association for Jazz Education (IAJE) (P.O. Box 724, Manhattan, KS 66505-0724, iaje.org) publishes a list of schools that offer degrees in jazz. The association is active in promoting the study and appreciation of jazz. It also publishes a journal and a newsletter.

Jazzmobile, Inc. was founded in 1964 by the jazz pianist/composer/educator Dr. Billy Taylor to instruct, present, propagate, and preserve jazz—"America's classical music"—as a national treasure. Jazzmobile produces concerts, festivals, and special events on a worldwide basis. The address is: Jazzmobile, 154 West 127th Street, New York, NY 10027, www.jazzmobile.org.

Here are some more good sources of information about the jazz scene:

allaboutjazz.com

allmusic.com

downbeat.com

Jazz Foundation of America
jazzfoundation.org

Jazz Journalist Association
jazzhouse.org

7

The Recording Industry

The record company is where all the action is. The company produces and promotes the artist, distributes and sells the product, and collects and pays the monies.

Record companies are corporations and therefore require the skills and talents of a large variety of professionals. Some companies are more on the creative side, while others are more corporate. Creative record companies are usually run by music people—musicians, arrangers, and producers who are very involved with producing the records and developing the artists. More corporate-structured companies are run by lawyers and accountants and depend on independent producers to record and develop the artists. However, the current trend for corporate companies is to have more executives with music backgrounds. The "Big 6"—SONY, RCA, Warner, EMI/Capitol, Polygram, and MCA—are large corporate record companies. Smaller companies, like A&M, Arista, and Geffen tend to be creatively oriented. However, Polygram purchased A&M, and MCA purchased Geffen Records, and ultimately Universal purchased Polygram and MCA.

There are more than two thousand record companies listed in *Billboard's International Buyers Guide* and approximately seven thousand recording artists listed in *Billboard's Talent and Touring Directory*. Many labels specialize in one or two categories with a minimum number of artists, while the bigger companies maintain a large number of artists in many categories. In the mid 1990s, Sony Records had a roster of approximately two hundred artists in all categories, while RCA had about one hundred; however, considering the increasing number of aspiring artists as well as new genres, and the fact that consumers are purchasing more and more CD players, with record sales reaching 942.5 million units shipped in 2000 (Recording Industry Association of America "Music Matters" report), those numbers could increase in the future.

Depending on the status of the artist, either the company will assign a producer (on-staff or independent), or the artist will choose the producer. Many superstars have their own publishing companies and demand to own all or part of the publishing rights of their songs.

The record industry is big business; records are selling in the millions with total sales in the billions of dollars. According to the RIAA "Music Matters" report, 2000 established an all-time high number of units shipped. The dollar volume for 2000 was $14.3 billion, which is a decline from the $14.6 billion volume of 1999. This decrease is attributed largely to new options provided by the Internet, which drove changes in consumer purchasing habits.

A 2000 RIAA statistical overview update report shows the following breakdown on percentage of dollars spent on the different types of music:

Rock	24.8%
Rap/Hip-Hop	12.9%
Pop	11.0%
Country	10.7%
R&B/Urban	9.7%
Religious	4.8%
Jazz	2.9%
Classical	2.7%
Sound Tracks	0.9%
Oldies	0.7%
Children's	0.6%
New Age	0.5%
Other	8.3%

Recording Industry Association of America (RIAA), 1330 Connecticut Avenue NW, Washington, D.C. 20036, www.riaa.org

The Making of a Record

It takes a record company and its whole staff to plan and coordinate the strategy necessary to make and sell a record. The artist and repertoire (A&R) department is headed by the vice president of A&R, who may also be a staff producer responsible for the productions of some of the major artists with the label. Under the vice president is the staff A&R producer, who is responsible for recording and producing albums and singles with assigned artists. The A&R department prepares budgets and handles the paperwork both for the department and for the recording sessions.

The director of the talent acquisitions department could also be considered a talent scout. It is that department's responsibility to find new artists, produce demos, and participate in the selection and signing of artists. The people who work in both of these departments must have a good ear and a feel for commercial songs and artists. They must be completely familiar with the music ratings charts and be tuned in to the styles and trends of the music world.

The artist, having been discovered by the director of talent acquisition and brought into the company with the approval of the entire A&R staff and its director, is then ready to begin planning the album. The A&R director, along with the producer (and possibly the artist's manager), plans the concept of the album and selects the songs. If the artist is also a songwriter, then some of her or his songs may be used.

The artist is given a budget, which is used to plan the number of musicians, arrangements, and studio time. The A&R manager then coordinates the session with the studio manager or traffic manager of the recording studio. For many years, record companies maintained their own in-house recording studios, but they have discontinued this practice and now use independent, outside studios for their recordings.

After the session is finished (recorded and mixed), the master is sent to the plant to be readied for production. The original tapes, discs, or hard drives are carefully filed away by the vault manager.

Meanwhile, back at the record company, the creative services department has been very busy. The vice president of creative services plans the budget and administers the advertising, art, publicity, and packaging. The advertising manager plans the advertising campaign and, according to the amount of exposure planned, selects the appropriate media. The media buyer then coordinates the advertising campaign with radio, television, trade magazines, and newspapers.

The art director supervises the project and assigns the work to the photographers, graphic artists, designers, and copywriters, who together prepare the CD cover and the ad layouts. The camera-ready artwork is sent to the printer and turned into CD covers, cassette covers, and inserts; these are shipped to the manufacturing plant and, together with the CDs and the cassette tapes, are assembled into the final product. While all this recording and drawing, printing, and pressing is going on, the product manager, the A&R department, and the artist's manager plan all the strategies involved with releasing the album. They coordinate the release date with the directors of promotion, marketing, public relations, and sales.

The director of artist development, along with the artist's manager and concert promoter, plan the live performances, the promotion tour, radio and television appearances, special concerts, and everything else that will make the public aware of the artist and the record. A record that doesn't get heard doesn't get sold, so the function of the promotion department is to make sure that the record gets on the air. The vice president of promotion is in charge of the directors of national promotion, regional promotion, and local promotion. Promotion personnel go into the field and work with radio station promotion directors and DJs on both the secondary stations and the major stations for airplay. The promotion people in the field build relationships with the local disc jockeys and record stores. They stimulate interest in the artist and report sales to the radio stations and to the tip sheets (a special trade paper that goes out to radio stations). They report all action to the trade papers, such as *Billboard* and *Variety*.

An artist's promotion tour usually includes a guest appearance on the local DJ's radio show, the local television show, and an appearance at the local record store to sign autographs; all of this is planned and coordinated by the promotion department. The director of press information, the publicist, and the director of marketing all work at securing press coverage and exposure.

Sales managers, merchandising managers, and distribution managers all work toward one end: to get the record to the consumer.

Large record companies work with many college promotion, and/or marketing departments and have a "college rep." He or she acts as an intern and is responsible for getting airplay on the college radio station and putting up posters that advertise the artist and the record.

The copyright administrator deals with publishers in matters of licenses, royalties, and copyrights. The vice president of business affairs negotiates with artists' managers, producers, and publishers. A musician with education or experience in sales, marketing, management, or business administration could get a good start in the music business with a record company. Record companies like to promote from within, as well as hire from within the field, and a job opening for a trainee might just be the start of a music career.

Record companies are all over the country, but the main concentration of companies is in New York, Nashville, and Los Angeles. The large companies have offices in all three cities, as well as small offices all around the country. These small offices operate much like the main office, and a job with a small office may lead to the main office.

There is very little turnover in the business, but there are job opportunities at the lower levels as well as the executive levels. Openings are sometimes advertised in the help-wanted ads in newspapers and in the trade magazines. Also, there are employment agencies that specialize in record and publishing company jobs. Trade papers that dispense music business information are *Billboard*, *Variety*, and the *Hollywood Reporter*.

Becoming a Recording Artist

The ultimate goal of nearly every musician and singer is to be a recording artist. The prestige of having a record and the exposure from TV, radio, and magazine promotion can improve the quality of bookings and attract the attention of agents and managers who can further an artist's career. A hit record can skyrocket an artist from total obscurity to international fame in a very short time. Getting a recording contract, however, is no easy matter, and getting a hit is almost impossible. Even a hit record has to be backed up with a dynamite act, a good video, a second and even a third hit in order to solidify the performer's career as a recording artist.

As a performing artist you can approach talent scouts with a demo by knocking on their doors or going through lawyers, managers, producers, or other artists who have gained the confidence of talent scouts. Talent scouts often travel to many cities to listen to an artist that a local promoter or disc jockey recommended. Live performance is extremely important in getting a record company interested in signing you, and in addition to sounding good, an artist must also look good.

Building a following and generating a lot of excitement can influence a record executive just as it can an audience. That's what the executive is looking for, an artist who can deliver on the promotion tour and sell records. The average life span of an unprepared artist is five years. That is why it is important to take the time to develop good performing skills by studying, practicing, and working in clubs.

The Internet

The digital era has opened up enormous possibilities for music on the Internet, and the Recording Industry Association of America (riaa.org) is striving to create a legitimate online market.

For the first time, major record companies are offering digital music downloads and, in fact, many new artists got additional exposure on the Internet that helped their careers. Groups such as They Might Be Giants and Ani Difranco, as well as established recording artists like Prince, have sold their music on the Internet.

However, some companies like Napster, Scour, and MP3.com have not respected artists' intellectual rights and have downloaded copyrighted music without compensating the artists.

In the year 2000, the U.S. Circuit Court of Appeals ruled that Napster must prevent users from gaining access to copyrighted content using its software.

The RIAA SoundByting (soundbyting.com) campaign has targeted more than four hundred colleges and universities to educate people to the fact that uploading and downloading copyrighted music without an artist's permission is illegal and hinders the development of a legitimate online music market.

The RIAA has also launched a program called SoundExchange, which is an outgrowth of the Digital Performance Rights Act. It uses precision technology to build a play-for-pay system for digital performances.

A musician who has a background in digital technology, computer skills, and/or copyright law, would be a valuable asset to the performers' unions—AFofM and AFTRA—and performance rights organizations—ASCAP, BMI, and SESAC—as well as to record companies and publishing companies.

Making the Demo

Before you make a demo, you should know exactly what you want it to show. For example, if your focus is the song, it takes one kind of demo; if it's the singing, the band, or the production, that takes another. Is it a song that requires a heavy drumbeat, or one that shows off the lyrics, the melody, or the arrangement? All of these factors must be considered and the session carefully planned before spending hard-earned money on a record date. If you have a unique, original, and exciting sound in a live performance, then that is what you have to capture in the studio. That's what makes a performer a recording artist. The demo, or demo-master, should sound as professional as possible so that the recording company will know exactly what you sound like on CD. You are the best judge of your sound by comparing the demo to the CDs already on the charts. If you show some promise of becoming a hit act, you might be able to make a deal with a studio owner. Many recording artists have received free studio time in exchange for a piece of the action. You might even produce yourself with your own money or with backers' money.

Once you have a finished master, you can approach the record companies with it. Some labels are willing to listen to a finished master rather than just a demo. If a company signs an artist on the strength of a demo, then they first have to start planning the album. However, a self-contained performer who writes his or her own songs and has a finished master may be more attractive to a record company.

Producers

The producer is the person responsible for making the CD. Some record companies have staff producers, and others contract the services of independent producers. An unknown artist signed to a recording contract would be assigned to a producer who would plan the album. However, the superstars have the advantage of choosing who will produce and what songs will be performed.

The 45 RPM 7″ single has long been phased out, and the single cassette taken its place. However, today's record business is completely CD oriented (the album as we once knew it—33⅓ RPM 12″ vinyl pressing—has also become obsolete and been replaced by the cassette tape and the CD). Besides the better quality of sound on the CD, it can hold up to 77 minutes of music, as opposed to the LP, which holds up to 43 minutes of music on both sides. From 1986 to 2000, CD sales increased from 53 million units to 942.5 million units.

At one time, a recording artist only had to come up with an "A" side and a "B" side (45 RPM 7″ single). Now that same artist has to come up with 10 to 12 songs to fill a CD. Instead of producing two songs (one per side), a producer has to come out with 10 to 12 songs. And with the competition today, each cut has to be a gem. That means 10 to 12 arrangements, more studio and mixing time, more musicians, more tape, and a lot more money.

A record producer is responsible for the production from start to finish, from the concept to the final mix, from the CD cover to the promotion, and from the pressing to the airplay. A producer must know the business and the creative side of music, have a good feel for what is commercial, have an understanding and love for music, and be willing to take chances. He or she must know how to budget a record date and deal with lawyers, contracts, publishers, record company executives, musicians, singers, songwriters, arrangers, engineers, managers, union regulations, and, most of all, artistic temperament.

Producers generally start out as engineers, composers, arrangers, studio musicians, artists, or professional managers, and they get their training on the job. Sometimes producers will use their own money, the record company's money, the artist's money, or an investor's money to produce a CD.

Producers generally earn a royalty on the record sales, and their initial fee can range from $5,000 to $40,000 or more, with some star producers earning $100,000 and more per album, plus points, usually 2 to 4 percent. The exact fee depends on the type of artist produced, the genre, and the status of the producer. The producer's fee is generally part of the whole production budget, which in the case of a superstar, can be in the millions. Many independent producers also own their own publishing companies and earn additional money by including songs from their catalogs on the CDs.

CD costs are extremely high, and the following is just a rough estimate of the kind of money it takes to produce and promote an artist today. A rock group can cost $250,000, and up, to produce. An established star can cost in the millions. However, production costs for a jazz artist's album can range from $75,000 to $500,000 to produce. Promotion costs can range from $50,000 to $500,000 and more, and this does not include graphics and manufacturing costs.

Then comes the music video. The minimum cost to produce a music video for a new band is at least $50,000 and up. The more established artists' budgets can be $500,000 and up, and the superstars spend $1,000,000 and more for their music videos. The music video has become an important asset to promoting an artist and his or her CD. In fact, in the early 1980s, the record industry was experiencing a recession, when along came MTV (Music Television). MTV immediately recaptured the interest of young audiences, and record sales began to rise. In some instances the visual is stronger than the music and the video can create the hit.

However, Music Television is reluctant to try a new recording artist; they prefer to play the videos of more established artists. A producer and a record company must have a lot of confidence in an artist before they start spending money on a video.

Control Room Engineers

A recording studio is divided into two areas. The studio is where the singers and musicians work. The other area is the control room. The two areas are separated by double plate glass windows so that both sides can see each other but no sound will penetrate. Communication is done through microphones and speakers. The studio is acoustically designed (angled walls and ceiling) so that certain frequencies do not cancel each other out, and certain areas are padded with sound-absorbing materials to prevent reverberation and penetration of sound from outside the studio.

The control room is where the console (mixing board), tape decks, computers, and other sophisticated recording equipment are located. The control room is operated by two engineers: one who operates the console and works directly under the producer, and one who operates the tape machines. Also on hand is a maintenance engineer whose responsibility it is to repair equipment in the event of a malfunction. The engineers set up the microphones, the musicians, and the baffles (devices that regulate the flow of sound). The engineers are usually assisted by a helper who sets up music stands, chairs, and headphones; plugs in cables; and goes for coffee. This helper is sometimes called a "go-fer."

The sound engineer must know how to translate the producer's ideas into buttons, dials, and switches in order to produce the quality of sound desired. Sometimes a recording session will last for many hours, and an engineer must have a lot of patience and stamina. An engineer must be able to work quickly and accurately under pressure, and since studio time is expensive, there is little room for errors. Imagine accidentally erasing a portion of a tape that took hours to record (after the orchestra has already left the studio). It can and has happened, and it is a very expensive mistake.

An engineer with a music background can be a valuable asset to a producer of popular or classical music recording sessions. Engineers work on staff, as well as freelance. A beginner (assistant engineer) would earn the minimum wage, while the salary for a seasoned professional can range from $40 to $80 or more an hour, with the superstar engineers earning in the six figures per year. It all depends upon location and status in the profession. Most engineers and assistants usually put in a lot of overtime when working on a project. The high cost of maintaining a studio (rent, staff, and maintenance) has caused many major record companies to close their in-house studios.

The availability of quality multitrack home recording equipment coupled with a computer, MIDI, and a bunch of synthesizers and samplers has made it possible for songwriters, singers, and musicians to do their productions in their home studios. This has taken a lot of work away from the smaller independent studios. However, new digital technology has created the compact disc, or CD, and with it a healthy future for the recording industry. Where there is new technology, there are new opportunities.

The CD is a 4¾″ disk digitally encoded with billions of pits that represent up to seventy-seven minutes of music on one side only. These pits are read by a laser beam stylus, then converted back into an analog signal, which is fed into a conventional amplifier and speakers to reproduce the recorded sound. However, that's where the difference is: The sound is pure, with no hiss or flutter. With a CD there's no surface noise, pops, clicks, or interference from dust, scratches, or skipping.

As more consumers purchase CD players, more and more CDs will have to be made available. Record producers and engineers will have to learn new techniques for digital recording. Many recording studios use DAT (digital audiotape) multitrack recording machines and hard-drive digital "direct-to-disc" technology, such as Pro-Tools and Synclavier, and then mix down to a DAT two-track stereo machine or to a CD. New music formats, such as the DVD-audio and the Super Audio CD (SACD), are the next wave of music technology that has to be learned. Many studios use automated mixing boards, and an engineer must know how to program the computer for this technology.

Professional Organizations

The Audio Engineering Society, Inc. (AES)
60 East Forty-second Street, Room 2520
New York, NY 10165
aes.org

The AES is devoted exclusively to audio technology, and its membership is made up of engineers, scientists, administrators, and technicians who deal with audio engineering and acoustics. The society holds conventions and seminars and publishes a journal that keeps its membership informed about new techniques, equipment, and technology.

The National Academy of Recording Arts and Sciences (NARAS)
3402 Pico Boulevard
Santa Monica, CA 90405
grammy.com

NARAS membership is made up of singers, musicians, producers, engineers, songwriters, composers, arrangers, and all the other craftspeople who are involved in the creative process of making records. Chapters are in Los Angeles, New York, Nashville, Chicago, Atlanta, San Francisco, and Memphis.

NARAS presents the annual Grammy Awards, and its members nominate and vote for the winners. NARAS offers seminars, scholarships, a newsletter, a journal, and specially priced, newly released CDs, tapes, and videos.

The oldest and most important NARAS program, first held in 1987 in New York City, is Grammy in the Schools, which provides high school students with information about recording industry careers both in front of and behind the microphone. It gives thousands of students the opportunity to interact with top industry professionals such as popular singers, songwriters, recording engineers, A&R reps, film composers, and others. The students are provided with insider information and a sixty-four-page *Career Handbook*. Grammy in the Schools events are held annually in urban areas across the country.

Write to the national office for the chapter near you.

Society of Motion Picture and Television Engineers (SMPTE)
595 West Hartsdale Avenue
White Plains, NY 10607
smpte.org

The membership of SMPTE is made up of professionals who work in the motion picture and television industry in the United States, Canada, and sixty other countries. They include engineers, technicians, producers, directors, people in sound recording, and all the other crafts that go into the business of film and video. SMPTE publishes a journal, a newsletter, and books, as well as sponsoring an annual technical conference.

Studio Singers

Studio singers are also recording artists. They are heard as background vocalists on tapes, CDs, film, and television, or as group singers and soloists in commercials and jingles. The very successful singers make a lot of money, but it's a competitive field, and very few people do the bulk of the work. A singer who is being used for his or her special sound can become very popular and get a lot of work; however, overexposure can burn someone out.

Producers and ad agencies cast a voice in the same manner that a casting director chooses an actor for a part. When a product is to be advertised for a certain market, they use a singer with the sound that will best represent their product in that market. For example, if a client wants to sell the product in an R&B market, then a singer with an R&B style and sound will be used.

However, a studio singer is a singer first and must have excellent sight-singing skills and knowledge of all musical styles, from classical to gospel. A studio singer must also have a good personality, work well with other singers, and be able to take direction. In addition, he or she must be a quick learner. It is critical to have a voice that records well, but even more important is the ability to blend well with other singers. Group singers go on and on. A good ear, good pitch, good intonation and diction, good microphone technique, and a good sense of rhythm, along with a wide range, flexibility, and a unique sound are important assets.

Advertising agency music directors, independent producers, and contractors usually use the same singers over and over again; however, they do keep demo tapes on file. Occasionally a producer will be looking for a unique or different sound, and a singer who is in the right place at the right time can be discovered! Ideally, a demo tape should contain real on-air commercials. Since a beginner does not have a track record, this is not possible. An alternative is to make up a demo tape from some of your best recorded performances, showing a good variety of your style, range, and flexibility, possibly adding some short spots to show the sound of your voice doing jingles.

A singer with access to a small multitrack MIDI studio could very well put together a demo. There are some studios with access to the actual music tracks of a commercial, without the voice. For a fee, they will overdub you as the singer and put together a demo tape.

At a seminar on jingle singing presented by AFTRA for its membership, the topic "the job market" was addressed by one of New York's top studio singers. Everyone had pad and pen ready to copy down a list of contacts, so that the next day they could be out cutting jingles. The speaker stood up and said, "The job market is wherever you can find it." How true that is. There are no ads or agents for studio work, so it takes determination, motivation, and being in the right place at the right time.

The telephone directory; *Shoot Commercial Production Directory* (BPI Communications, 770 Broadway, New York, NY 10003, www.bpicomm.com); *Fashion and Print Directory* and the *Film and Television Directory* (Peter Glenn Publications, pgdirect.com); and the *Black Book* (a very expensive set of books on the advertising industry) contain lists of advertising agencies and music commercial producers (sometimes called music houses). Making the rounds of these offices is the best way to introduce yourself. However, unless you've been recommended by someone close to the producer, you can expect to be turned away on your first visit. A lot of persistence and self-confidence are needed to show your enthusiasm so that sooner or later you will be given an opportunity to show your stuff.

Studying voice or sight-singing with a teacher who does studio work or who has contacts with a producer or a vocal contractor might help. Belonging to professional organizations made up of singers and/or songwriters is another way to meet the people who may help you be in the right place at the right time.

Singing in a nightclub or musical theater is a good showcase. Inviting music directors, contractors, and producers to see your performance is bringing the right people to the right place. Even if they don't show up, at least they will become familiar with your name and know that you are a working professional.

Recording demos for songwriters and publishers and singing back-up vocals play a very important part in becoming known in the business. Working among professionals who are studio musicians and singers will bring leads, tips, and introductions. Breaking into studio work is a full-time occupation. In most cases, as mentioned earlier, sight-singing skills are essential, and if sight-singing is not one of your strong points, then start studying, preferably with a professional studio singer who can also guide your career.

AFTRA's 2001 national pay scale for studio singers was $220.00 each for a soloist or duo. For groups of 3 to 5 singers, $162.05

each; for 6 to 8 singers, $143.40 each; and for 9 or more, $127.25 each per session. A session is one and a half hours during which one spot, up to ninety seconds can be recorded. Each additional spot is considered a session. The residuals (payment for reruns) are based on how the commercials are aired (television, radio; national, regional, or local) and how many times they are aired. A top studio singer can earn a yearly salary into the six figures. Studio singers belong to the American Federation of Television and Radio Artists (AFTRA) and the Screen Actors Guild (SAG). Studio singers can work wherever there is a studio, and that can be anywhere in the country; however, the main concentration of work is in New York, Chicago, Los Angeles, and Nashville.

Studio Musicians

Studio musicians are recording artists, too. Their special and unique talents are heard on records, commercials, jingles, in film, television, and in background music. Many of the studio musicians got their start by doing demos, being part of a famous entertainer's back-up band, playing in a Broadway pit orchestra, being radio or television staff musicians, or by having been recording artists themselves.

A studio musician must have excellent playing and reading skills. Excessive mistakes are not tolerated. He or she must have a special and unique sound that a producer needs. The horns and string players are always reading parts (music). And even though the rhythm players have parts to read, they are sometimes hired for their "feel" for the type of music being recorded. In Nashville the session players use what is called the Nashville numbers system. It simply means that the chords are called by their numbers and not their names. For example, C, A minor, D minor, and G7 will look like this: 1, 6, 2, 5. *The Nashville Numbers System* explains the system well (see Bibliography).

Studio work is booked by contractors. Usually one contractor will book the whole session; however, on larger sessions a second contractor may be hired to book the string players, and a third contractor may book the singers. Producers and composers have their favorite players and generally know who can deliver a special sound that may be needed; they will ask the contractor to book a certain musician or singer for a particular record, jingle, or film sound track.

Studio musicians have to be very flexible and able to play many different styles, as well as double on other instruments in the same family. Patience, a good personality, a positive attitude, and the ability to work well with other musicians is very important. A studio musician must also be able to take direction, and the really good ones are able to contribute ideas and musical suggestions to the producer.

Musicians belong to a local of the American Federation of Musicians of the United States and Canada (AFM). The national pay scale for a basic regular session is $313.45 (plus pension and health contributions) for three hours in which no more than fifteen minutes of music are recorded. Leaders and contractors get double scale. A one-hour jingle session will pay $100.00 per musician and double for the leader (plus pension and health contributions) with two or more musicians, for no more than three national spots and a total of three minutes of music to be recorded. Film, television, radio, and TV commercials and recordings each have a different pay scale. Symphonic recording also has a different pay scale. Some musicians who have a special or unique sound and are in demand are usually paid double scale and sometimes more. (This extra pay is referred to as "overscale.")

Economics and cutbacks can reduce the amount of work available in the recording studio. Electronic synthesizers and samplers have replaced the need for drummers, string players, and horn players for certain sessions. Some producers record the rhythm tracks in this country and go to Europe to record the strings and horns. For the price of an airplane ticket and a hotel, they can save thousands of dollars on the musicians.

Some pianists have become keyboard players; they specialize in programming and performing on synthesizer and samplers (also called programmers). Drummers, too, have learned to work on electronic drums, sequencers, and drum machines. A musician who is employed to play an electronic musical device on a multitracking session usually receives an hourly rate above union scale.

The National Academy of Recording Arts and Sciences has a Heroes Award, which honors people in the recording industry, including studio musicians, for outstanding achievements. Some musicians—who also compose, arrange, orchestrate, and produce—start their own production companies. Or they work as music directors for advertising agencies, as A&R directors with record companies, or as professional managers for publishing companies.

The main concentration of activity for studio musicians is in New York, Nashville, Los Angeles, and Chicago. Other areas like Toronto, Shreveport, Muscle Shoals, Atlanta, Miami, and Memphis also have their share of studio work. Although each area has a variety of work, New York and Chicago have more jingle-recording sessions. Nashville has more country and pop recording sessions, Los Angeles has more feature film and television recording sessions.

8

Extending Career Choices

Teaching

Music education is a two-sided coin: It is a subject to be learned for its own sake (theory, singing, and instruments), and it is a tool for learning. Over the years studies have shown that young children who participated in music training have a definite advantage over those who did not. Academically, they achieved higher grades in math, reading, and writing; they were good listeners and had a better capacity for comprehension. They developed a higher degree of confidence, imagination, and creativity. This means that music is an important factor in the development and training of children.

Being taught rhythms, melody, music appreciation, and group performance allows students to develop awareness and insights about themselves and about the world around them. In fact, recent studies have shown again that students who studied music did better in math, had higher SATs, had low lifetime and current substance abuse issues, and that music lessons actually stimulated brain growth.[1] However, budget cutbacks in recent years have limited the opportunities in music education in the public schools. Despite all this research and the statistics showing the importance of music education, it is still not considered a core subject in many school systems.

Music education in New York City was dealt a devastating blow in the mid-1970s. Budget cutbacks eliminated many music programs, and along with it, music teachers were let go. However, in 1997, the Mayor in collaboration with the Board of Education, developed a program called Project Arts and began funding schools with $75 million a year to restore their arts programs (including music).

In fact the July/August 1999 issue of *Allegro* (Local 802, Musicians Union newspaper) carried an article entitled "Board of Education Seeking Teachers for Public School Music Programs."

Project Arts works in collaboration with the Save the Music Foundation, VH-1, the International Music Products Association (NAMM), the American Music Conference (AMC), the National Academy of Recording Arts and Sciences (NARAS), and other music and educational groups to promote music education on a national level as well. For more information on Project Arts and Save the Music Foundation, visit: amcmusic.com, vh1.com, or nycenet.edu/projectarts.

Nancy Shankman, Director of Arts Education, New York City Board of Education, said that they hope that the New York City initiative to reinstate arts and music education in the school sys-

---

1. "Music Makes the Difference: Music, Brain Development, and Learning." The National Association for Music Education (MENC), 2000.

tem will be a model for all school systems nationally, as well as for New York State.

A music teacher is a teacher first, and he or she should have a degree in education. Some teachers are hired from the field, but with the tight job market, the more education you have, the better chance you'll have of getting a position.

Elementary School

According to the Bureau of Labor Statistics, in 1998, 1.9 million teachers worked in kindergarten and elementary schools. The job opportunities are expected to increase 10 to 20 percent, as with all occupations, through the year 2008.

Elementary school teachers must have a bachelor's degree from an institution with an approved teacher education program. They must also be certified by the state. For example, in order to receive permanent certification by the New York State Education Department and the New York City School System, a teacher must also have a master's degree and/or eighteen credits in education. Check with your state's education department for its guidelines. Information on certification requirements is available from the superintendent of schools of any state department of education, or a certification advisory committee.

Besides the basic music courses, an elementary music teacher should also study the educational techniques of Orff, Suzuki, Kodaly, and Dalcroze. He or she must have patience, enjoy working and communicating with children, be creative, and have good leadership qualities. Piano, guitar, and singing skills are very important for an elementary school teacher. According to the American Federation of Teachers, the average salary of all public elementary and secondary school teachers in 1997–98 was

$39,300, with higher salaries in the Northeast and the West. Teachers in private schools generally earn less than those in public schools.

Secondary School

Secondary school teachers, like elementary school teachers, must have a bachelor's degree and must be certified by the state. About 1.4 million secondary or high school teachers were employed in 1998.

According to Market Data Retrieval's Spring 2001 catalog (schooldata.com), the number of educators in this country's public and private schools in all grades (K–12) is 3.4 million. Of those 3.4 million teachers, 119,064 are listed as music educators. This means that approximately 3.5 percent are music teachers, which is down from the 4.8 percent reported by the National Center for Education Statistics (nces.ed.gov) in the early 1990s. However, with the current Project Arts initiative in the New York City school system, along with the national Save the Music Foundation campaign, the percentage of music teachers should increase in the future.

In a secondary school, the music program depends upon the size of the school budget. In a small school, one or two instructors may have the responsibility for all the music programs. In a large school, several music teachers may be on staff, each with a specialty. Where a school has a large enrollment, it is possible to have a band, an orchestra, and a choir.

School music teachers must be qualified to teach (and coach) voice and instruments, as well as conduct and direct the band, orchestra, and choir. Music appreciation, music history, theory, and ensemble work are also taught in the secondary schools.

Besides the basic courses, a music teacher must be prepared to direct a school musical play, prepare the band for the school's sporting events, and plan the music for school dances. A high school teacher must enjoy working with teenagers, have patience and an understanding of their nature, and have a congenial personality and good leadership qualities.

Teachers often work on community projects and work part-time in night clubs, resorts, club dates, private teaching, church music, or in music therapy programs.

College/University

According to the National Center for Education Statistics, in 1995 about 932,000 people were employed to teach various subjects in the nation's 4,064 colleges and universities. About three out of ten worked part-time.

College and university teachers are classified as professors, associate professors, assistant professors, and instructors. Instructors must have at least a master's degree, but because of the competition, a doctorate degree is more often required to get an appointment. Some states require several years of public school teaching experience before granting a college or university position.

Student enrollment is projected to rise from 14.6 million in 1998 to 16.1 million in 2008. Employment opportunities for college and university faculty are expected to increase faster than the average through 2008, based on the increase in enrollment, with additional openings arising as faculty members retire.

Earnings vary according to faculty rank and type of institution, geographic area, and field. According to a 1998–99 survey by the American Association of University Professors, salaries for full-time faculty averaged $56,300. By rank, the salary averages for professors was $72,700; associate professors, $53,200; assistant professors, $43,800; instructors, $33,400; and lecturers, $37,200.

In colleges, universities, and conservatories, the music teacher is a specialist and is hired as such. He or she teaches a specific instrument or specializes in harmony and theory, sight-singing, composition, orchestration, music history, conducting, voice, or other music and music-related courses.

The National Research Council, an independent organization chartered by Congress, conducted a comprehensive four-year study called Research-Doctorate Programs in the United States. It studied 3,634 academic programs at 274 institutions (105 private and 169 public). The resulting scholastic ratings for doctorate programs in music were published in the September 13, 1995 issue of the *New York Times*. The eleven best programs, listed from highest to lowest, follow:

Harvard
University of Chicago
University of California, Berkeley
CUNY Graduate School
Yale
Princeton
University of Pennsylvania
University of Rochester
University of Michigan

University of Illinois
Cornell University

The Chronicle of Higher Education (1255 Twenty-third Street NW, Washington, D.C. 20037, chronicle.com) has a want-ad section that advertises openings in colleges and universities for teachers, administrators, and directors.

Some colleges and universities have music departments that have a specialty in music education in addition to the usual undergraduate music curriculum. For example, Dr. Bernard Shockett, chairman of the music department at Lehman College/CUNY, recognized a need in professional musicians who wanted to teach music in the school system, but had studied privately, never completed their music degree, and/or were busy with their performing careers.

Dr. Shockett developed a program, in association with Local 802, AFM, designed for professional musicians' schedules, whereby they could continue to work as performers as they earned their B.S. (Bachelor of Science) degrees in music and M.A.T. (Masters of Arts in Teaching) degrees in music education. The program, dubbed The Lehman-802 Program, has been successful for the past thirty years.

Where to Get Training and Information

According to the NASM, as of July 2001, there were approximately 586 colleges and universities that offered music education. The National Association of Schools of Music (NASM, 11250 Roger Bacon Drive, Suite 21, Reston, VA 20190) has available a directory ($20) that lists accredited institutions and major degree programs (visit artsaccredit.org).

For information on college and university teaching, write to the following organizations:

American Association of University Professors
1012 Fourteenth Street NW, Suite 500
Washington, D.C. 20005-3465
aaup.org

National Council for Accreditation of Teacher Education (NCATE)
2010 Massachusetts Avenue NW, Suite 200
Washington, D.C. 20036-1023
ncate.org

Information about teachers' unions can be obtained by writing to the following address:

American Federation of Teachers
555 New Jersey Avenue NW
Washington, D.C. 20001-2079
aft.org

For general teaching information, contact:

Division of Human Resources
Office of Educational Staff Recruitment
New York City Board of Education
65 Court Street
Brooklyn, NY 11201
1-800-TEACH-NY
www.teachny.com

National Education Association
1201 Sixteenth Street NW
Washington, D.C. 20036-3290
nea.org

A Free Internet Teacher Placement Service can be found at teachers-teachers.com.

The following organizations have information, publications, seminars, conventions, and music educator members:

American Council on Education
One Dupont Circle NW
Washington, D.C. 20036-1193
acenet.edu

American Music Conference
5790 Armada Drive
Carlsbad, CA 92008
amc-music.com

American Musicological Society
201 South Thirty-fourth Street
Philadelphia, PA 19104-6313
sas.upenn.edu/music/ams

American Orff-Schulwerk Association
P.O. Box 391089
Cleveland, OH 44139-8089
aosa.org

American String Teachers Association
National School Orchestra Association
4153 Chain Bridge Road
Fairfax, VA 22030
astaweb.com

College Music Society
202 West Spruce Street
Missoula, MT 59802
music.org

Music Educators National Conference (MENC)
1806 Robert Fulton Drive
Reston, VA 20191
menc.org

Music Teachers National Association
The Carew Tower
441 Vine Street, Suite 505
Cincinnati, OH 45202-2811
mtna.org

National Association of Schools of Music
11250 Roger Bacon Drive, Suite 21
Reston, VA 20190
artsaccredit.org

Organization of American Kodaly Educators
1612 Twenty-ninth Avenue South
Moorhead, MN 56560
oake.org

Suzuki Association of the Americas
P.O. Box 17310
Boulder, CO 80308
suzukiassociation.org

Private Instruction

Teaching privately can be a wonderful way of earning a living. It can be done in your own home, in the student's home, or in a studio. Some private teachers rent studio space from a local music shop or work at a small music school. You can teach full or part time, depending, of course, on economics, population, and competition in your area.

A very important side effect of teaching is that you constantly polish your own talents by keeping in touch with your roots. It's also a good way to become known among your peers. The most gratifying reward from teaching is watching your students learn and grow from your willingness to share your knowledge and experience. The most popular instruments presently are the piano, the accordion, the guitar, and voice.

If the local schools are large enough to have a good music program, you'll find many children wanting to learn band instruments as well. Trumpet, clarinet, saxophone, flute, violin, and drums are very popular instruments. Your teaching schedule will probably start around 3:00 in the afternoon, when the school day ends.

Fees for private teaching range from $25 to $75 per hour, depending on your geographical location, instrument, status in the business, and the market.

If you find a large number of people interested in studying one instrument, you might explore the possibility of group classes. A studio that also carries instruments, accessories, and sheet music, and does instrument repairs, can be a good business in the right location.

Local music shops sometimes advertise for teachers in the local newspapers help-wanted columns. A teacher wanting to start a private practice can send out flyers; advertise in a trade paper or local newspaper, school, church, or community bulletin board; and hang up a shingle.

Here is a list of organizations that dispense information and publications related to private teaching:

American Accordion Association
580 Kearny Avenue
Kearny, NJ 07032
www.ameraccord.com

National Association of Teachers of Singing
6406 Merrill Road, Suite B
Jacksonville, FL 32277
www.nats.org

The National Guild of Piano Teachers
808 Rio Grande Street
Austin, TX 78701
www.pianoguild.com

New York Singing Teachers Association
212-579-2461
www.nysta.org

The Superintendent of Documents has a booklet entitled *Starting a Business*. For a free catalog send a self-addressed, stamped envelope to the Consumer Information Center, P.O. Box 100, Pueblo, CO 81002; 1-888-878-3256; www.pueblo.gsa.gov.

Adult Education

Evening adult education centers offer courses in everything from sewing to socializing, including music: writing it, performing it, and appreciating it. There are classes in piano, guitar, singing, songwriting, opera, and musical theater. A teacher who can create an interesting program might be able to attract enough students to fill a classroom and supplement her or his income.

Training Aids

Another area open to teachers is the development of teaching materials. Educational materials—such as handbooks on teaching and music, and audio and video training programs—have to be developed and produced. Workshops, lectures, and clinics on music are all possible sources of employment. Possible topics include demonstrations of musical instruments, or lectures on music history, new techniques, or career opportunities.

Band Director

The band director is a conductor and the person responsible for musical extravaganzas at football games. There are about as many band directors as there are colleges, universities, and high schools. Some of the larger universities employ two, three, or even four band directors. The College Band Directors National Association (University of Texas, P.O. Box 8028, University Station, Austin,

TX 78713-8028, cbdna.org) has approximately 1,050 members and estimates that there are about 2,000 college band directors.

Although a band director is primarily a conductor, he or she is required to have a degree in music education. Since a degree in music education does not concentrate on preparing someone for conducting, it is up to the individual to be self-motivated and take additional courses in performance and conducting. Most large universities with a good band program can prepare someone for a career in band directing.

The difference between a band director and an orchestra conductor is the instrumentation and the repertoire. A band is made up of brass, woodwinds, and percussion, and the repertoire is more contemporary and generally in a march tempo. Band directors work with students, teaching them music as the students learn to play their instruments.

Band directors usually start at the high school level and work their way up to a university position after gaining the necessary experience. Depending on the size of the school, their responsibilities may include producing whole shows, from creating the concept to writing the arrangements, and from designing the marching routines to staging the band's performance.

Salaries are commensurate with those of teachers, but in a larger school situation where there are extra shows and concerts, a band director has the opportunity to earn extra money. Guest conducting, clinics, workshops, lectures, and private teaching can also add to a band director's income.

There are better job opportunities in a high growth area, but there are sometimes up to fifty applicants for one job opening. The *Chronicle of Higher Education* (1255 Twenty-third Street NW, Washington, D.C. 20037, chronicle.com) has a want-ad section that sometimes lists openings for band directors.

Musicologist

A musicologist works very closely with lawyers, publishers, advertising agencies, record companies, composers, and songwriters in matters of copyright infringement. They must have a strong background in music history and music theory, be familiar with copyright law and the legal language, as well as have the skill to write detailed analytical reports. They are called upon to make a comparison of musical compositions in alleged plagiarism cases and, therefore, must be able to read and transcribe music with great accuracy. Since their research, testimony, and expertise must be credible in a court of law, a Ph.D. or comparable experience is most desirable, and having access to recordings, record archives, and other pertinent source materials is extremely important.

Employment opportunities are limited. Musicology is an area of the music industry that requires a combination of skills that are not just musical, such as: people skills, extensive writing skills, computer skills, and the ability, patience, and tenacity to search through reams of reference materials. In some cases, vocal and/or instrumental performance skills are called upon when it is necessary to demonstrate a melody, a rhythmic, or a harmonic pattern in the presentation of a comparison analysis of a composition. A musicologist is also called upon to make a comparison analysis of sampled sounds, which are prevalent in today's music. Sampling is a high-tech digital computer method of recording a snippet of another artist's sound or a phrase from his or her performance, and using it as part of a different recording. Therefore, a musicologist must also be very familiar with the technology of sampling, as well as with the sounds and performances of recording artists and their recordings.

The majority of work for a musicologist today is in the major music centers: New York, Los Angeles, Nashville, and Chicago. Salaries are commensurate with a person's ability and reputation in the industry.

Music Librarian

A music librarian must love music and enjoy working with records, music books, and scores. Music librarians work in public libraries, conservatories, college/university libraries, the Library of Congress, symphony orchestras, opera companies, licensing agencies, publishing companies, radio and television stations, music preparation houses, and sheet music retailers. Necessary skills include being able to read a score, music copying, microfilming, cataloging, operating a computer, binding, typing, restoring, filing, and even speaking a foreign language. A good knowledge of the recordings and repertoire of classical, ethnic, jazz, and popular music is necessary.

Most public and academic libraries require a master's degree in library science (M.L.S.), preferably from an American Library Association accredited school, along with a master's degree in music (M.M.). As of 1998, there were fifty-six universities and colleges that offered an accredited M.L.S. A list of schools is available from the Music Library Association at musiclibraryassoc.org.

Working as a librarian for a symphony orchestra or opera company requires the ability to read a score, copy off parts and add notations, coordinate the purchase or rental of compositions for upcoming performances, and distribute and collect the parts for the rehearsals and the performances. In smaller orchestras, this job is usually done by one of the musicians.

A music librarian at a radio station is responsible for cataloging and filing all the records and tapes. He or she is sometimes referred to as the music director and works with the program director in selecting music for the various shows.

Working conditions for music librarians are pleasant, but the job market is tight. Openings depend on turnover. According to the Bureau of Labor Statistics, the median annual earnings of librarians in 1998 were $38,470. The middle 50 percent earned between $30,440 and $48,130. The lowest 10 percent earned less than $22,970, and the highest 10 percent earned more than $67,810. Median annual earnings in industries employing the largest number of librarians in 1997 were as follows: elementary schools, $38,900; colleges and universities, $38,600; local government, $32,600. The average annual salary for all librarians in the federal government (nonsupervisory, supervisory, and managerial positions) was $56,400 in 1999.

The Music Library Association maintains a placement service along with a publication that keeps its members informed. There are approximately two thousand members in MLA, and an additional one thousand subscribers to its publication. For more information write to the Music Library Association, c/o A–R Editions, Inc., 8551 Research Way, Suite 180, Middleton, WI 53562, musiclibraryassoc.org.

Music Critic

A music critic is a musician first and a reporter second. He or she must love music and writing about it. A critic must have a good ear; a well-rounded knowledge of all music styles, both old and new; and a familiarity with the standard repertoire. The ability to play an instrument, read music, and follow a score is essential for good criticism. A knowledge of the history and background of the style of music being reviewed is also important. A critic must have good writing skills and be able to express in words what he or she has heard in sound.

Critics work for newspapers and magazines and should be able to write in a style that is entertaining, stimulating, informative, and understandable to readers. A critic must know the audience for whom he or she is writing.

Presently there is one school that offers courses in music criticism; however, workshops and seminars are sponsored by the Music Critics Association (51 Primrose Circle, Princeton, NJ 08450, mcana.org). The association has 180 members and holds an annual meeting, usually at a major musical event.

Becoming a music critic takes self-motivation and on-the-job training. Someone wanting to become a music critic could write free articles for a college newspaper or a small community paper. After gaining some experience and credits, he or she could try to get work as a freelance writer or as a stringer (freelance reporter). Eventually these assignments might lead to a job as an assistant critic. The job market is very tight. Many college and university music teachers work part-time as stringers to supplement their incomes.

Since a music critic is a reporter, the salaries are negotiated by the American Newspaper Guild, and according to the Bureau of Labor Statistics, the median annual earnings of reporters and correspondents were $23,400 in 1997. The middle 50 percent earned between $17,500 and $35,600. The lowest 10 percent earned less than $12,900, and the highest 10 percent earned more than $55,600 a year.

Religious Music

Religious music offers opportunities for music directors, organists, choir directors, and singers. Some jobs are full-time and some are part-time. In order to have a career in religious music, you must enjoy playing the organ and working with a choir. But most importantly, you must have a good feel for and understanding of religious music. According to the Bureau of Labor Statistics, the median annual earnings of musicians and singers and related workers were $30,020 in 1998. Earnings depend on the professional status of the individual, as well as geographical location and hours worked. The more successful musicians and singers can earn far more than the median earnings indicated above.

Catholic Service

Before the early 1960s, the only music played in the Catholic church was traditional, with the mass delivered in Latin. However, the mass is now in English, and contemporary music has been introduced into the Catholic church. Folk, rock, and jazz masses have become commonplace.

Training

Choosing a college or university that specializes in organ and church music is very important. That can be discussed with your clergy or your teacher. It would be a good idea to combine your music education with business, as well as other performing arts courses.

The National Association of Schools of Music directory lists accredited colleges and universities along with their degree programs. Schools that offer instruction in religious music can be found in this directory. It is available from the National Association of Schools of Music, 11250 Roger Bacon Drive, Suite 21, Reston, VA 20190, or at artsaccredit.com.

There are many organizations that have seminars, workshops, and publications geared to inform and educate as well as maintain and improve the standards of organ, chorale, and church music.

Minister of Music

The minister (or director) of music handles the responsibilities of all the music and may have a choirmaster and an organist under her or his supervision. Besides the duties of supervising the music, a director may have to work with community projects, youth and senior citizen projects, and business administration. In some congregations, the music director is also the organist and the choir director.

The minister of music must have a background in church liturgy, harmony and theory, Gregorian chant, keyboard, choir, conducting, composition, hymns, and traditional music as well as contemporary music styles. He or she also needs some business and administrative abilities and a well-rounded knowledge of the arts.

There is no substitute for experience, and working with a music director, singing in the choir, and assisting the organist can provide valuable on-the-job training. In order to be a church organist, you must be able to read music, accompany singers and choirs, and perform as a soloist. Besides technique and a thorough knowledge of harmony and theory, the organist must also be familiar with the liturgical hymns and the repertoire from Gregorian chant to contemporary. The ability to improvise is also an asset.

A church organist sometimes freelances from one congregation to another. For example, you may perform for a Catholic service one day, accompany a choir in a Protestant church the next, then play for a Jewish service in a synagogue. The more knowledge you have of the needs of the different denominations, the more versatile you can be.

The organist is on call for weddings and funerals. This is an added source of income, and the fee is approximately $100 to $200 per service, depending on the congregation. Working outside the church can also supplement an income.

Choir Directors

A choir director must have a good knowledge of voice, vocal ranges, piano and organ, conducting, harmony and theory, arranging, Gregorian chant, hymns, liturgy, and the standard as well as the contemporary church repertoire. Besides the technical training, a choir director must have a good feel for religious music and a talent for blending voices.

Some congregations hire professional singers to work as soloists or to be part of the chorus. Some choruses are professional, and some are a mixture of professional singers and members of the congregation. Others are completely nonprofessionals; it all depends on the budget and the size of the congregation. An organist and a choir director must know how to handle both professional and nonprofessional singers.

Singers

A singer must have a good background in harmony and theory, Gregorian chant, liturgy, and hymns. Sight-singing skills are essential, since singers work in different denominations and are often introduced to new and different literature. A singer must also have the ability to sing in other languages, such as Latin, Italian, French, Spanish, Hebrew, German, and Greek.

Some wedding and funeral services use staff singers; however, outside vocalists are hired from time to time, depending on the situation. Fees range from $100 to $200. Singers also earn a living as voice teachers and vocal coaches or working in opera companies, musical theater, community projects, music therapy programs, club dates, nightclubs, or recording sessions.

Cantors

Cantors are singers that lead the Jewish service by chanting the prayers. Cantors work on a full-time or part-time basis, depending on the size of the congregation and the budget. Cantors also supplement their income by conducting the chorus and teaching Hebrew, Bible, and religion to the young, as well as preparing them for their bar mitzvah.

Study to become a cantor is done at the Cantorial Institute, which is part of the Jewish Theological Seminary, the Hebrew Union College, or Yeshiva University. The course of study includes Hebrew, religion, the Bible, and history of Jewish music, in addition to sight-singing, harmony, theory, vocal repertoire, style, all the prayer chants, and cantillation of the Torah. Studying voice is usually done privately with a teacher outside the school.

Gospel Music

Gospel music is a big part of the music industry. Some record and publishing companies specialize only in gospel music, and record sales are in the millions. Live gospel concerts draw thousands of fans, while TV and radio audiences can number in the millions. Gospel music comes in a variety of musical styles and employs many singers, instrumentalists, songwriters, composers, conductors, and arrangers.

Billboard, the music business weekly magazine, has feature sections on gospel music. News and business are discussed, along with a chart showing the record sales of gospel music. Buyers of religious music make up 4.8 percent of the market.

Organizations

American Guild of Organists
475 Riverside Drive, Suite 1260
New York, NY 10115
www.agohq.org

Cantors Assembly
3080 Broadway, Suite 613
New York, NY 10027
cantors.org

Gospel Music Association
1205 Division Street
Nashville, TN 37203
www.gospelmusic.org

The Hymn Society of America
Boston University School of Theology
745 Commonwealth Avenue
Boston, MA 02215-1401
hymnsociety.org

National Forum for Greek Orthodox Church Musicians
1700 North Walnut, Suite 302
Bloomington, IN 47404
ww2.goarch.org/goa/institutions/musicians

Music Therapy

If you've ever entertained in a prison, hospital, or a nursing home and you've witnessed your music bringing a smile to people's faces, then you've seen some of the therapeutic value of music. Music can get people to the center of the floor and dancing, or just put them in a romantic mood. Play a favorite song and watch someone's mood change as you stir up an old memory.

Music goes beyond just entertainment. Coupled with the science and art of healing, it becomes a useful tool in diagnosing and treating mental and physical illnesses. Music therapy has existed since the beginning of civilization, and yet only recently has it become recognized as a valid method of treatment by the modern medical profession. The use of music therapy came into focus around 1950, and it is still a new and growing field.

There are seventy colleges and universities that have accredited programs in music therapy. Nineteen of those award master's degrees, and seven award master's degrees and doctorates. The course of study is music therapy, anthropology, sociology, psychology, music, and general studies. Training is completed under the supervision of a registered music therapist. There are approximately 165 approved training and internship facilities in the United States.

Music therapists work with physicians and psychiatrists in mental institutions, geriatric centers, day-care centers, clinics for physically handicapped children, civilian and veterans' hospitals, and correctional institutions. According to the American Music Therapy Association (8455 Colesville Road, Suite 1000, Silver Spring, MD 20910-3392, musictherapy.org), there are approximately 6,000 people working in the profession. Of these, about 4,000 are members of the association, and approximately 4,500 are certified as music therapists. Salaries range from $25,000 to $80,000, and even with the economy and budget cuts, the job market seems to be healthy.

A music therapist should know how to play the piano, the guitar, other stringed instruments, wind instruments (like the recorder), and percussion and rhythm instruments. A therapist must enjoy working with people and have a desire to help them. Besides good physical and mental health, a therapist must have imagination, stamina, and a good sense of humor.

A music therapist uses playing and teaching instruments; singing, composing, and writing songs; as well as playing recordings to bring about a change in a patient. The process may involve using soothing, dissonant, or ethnic music to stir up emotions and draw them out. Playing an instrument can restore the patient's coordination, and singing can help overcome speech and breathing problems. Using group music activities helps patients build confidence and become aware of themselves and the world around them. Observing, diagnosing, and treating with music can restore mental and physical health. A therapist works with small and large groups and sometimes on a one-to-one basis.

A directory of schools and training facilities is available from the American Music Therapy Association. It includes a list of accredited colleges and universities. Volunteer and part-time help is needed in summer programs, drug and alcohol rehabilitation centers, hospitals, nursing homes, and mental institutions. Working in a summer music therapy program should give you a good idea of whether this is a career for you. Openings are sometimes advertised in the help-wanted section of the newspaper.

Military Music

The five branches of the military that offer opportunities for musicians and singers are the army, the navy, the air force, the marines, and the coast guard. Together they represent approximately 102 bands stationed in and around the United States and all over the world. The army has special bands stationed in the Washington, D.C. area: the U.S. Army Band, Pershing's Own, and the U.S. Army Field Band. The navy, the air force, and the marines each have one special band stationed in Washington. Their responsibilities range from parades and ceremonies to playing for dances at the White House.

The music requirements for a position in one of these special bands are very high, and auditions are arranged only when there is a vacancy. Also, a security clearance is necessary because the bands perform in and around the White House and come into close contact with the President. In fact, the marine corps band is called the President's Own. There is also a special band at each military academy and one on Paris Island.

The music ranges from symphonic to march and ceremonial to dance. The bands vary in size from a large symphony orchestra of about 40 to 251 pieces to an 18-piece dance band to a small combo. Military performance groups are classified as symphony orchestra, concert band, stage band, field band, dance band, chorus, chorale, drum-and-bugle corps, drum-and-fife corps, string ensemble, soloists, jazz-rock-country-blues combos, and special entertainment groups. The air force has a famous chorus known as The Singing Sergeants.

There are approximately 50 army bands, 14 navy bands, 14 marine bands, 20 air force bands, and 1 coast guard band. They are classified as premier, special, and field.

Before you consider the military, you must understand that the military book of rules comes first. There is a certain code of dress, grooming, and discipline that you must be able to adjust to. Also, there is the term of enlistment, depending on the branch of service. It can be from a minimum of three to four years to as long as you want. If you choose, it can be your whole career.

If you are not assigned to one of the special bands, it could mean being stationed far away from your home, even overseas. Some of the special bands and choruses go on tours as representatives of the United States Armed Forces and entertain all over the world. If you like to travel, that could be a positive aspect of music in the military.

The military needs men and women instrumentalists, singers, composers, arrangers and orchestrators, copyists, conductors, music directors, librarians, accompanists, teachers, and instrument repair technicians. An applicant must have a musical specialty, a background in harmony and theory, the ability to read music, and the ability to meet the standard enlistment requirements before auditioning. An audition can be set up through your local recruiter, or directly with the commander of a special band. Depending on the applicant's qualifications, the audition may be in Washington, D.C., or at a local installation.

Upon completion of basic training, which can be from eight to twelve weeks, depending on the branch of the service, the musician is then sent to the military school of music in Norfolk, Virginia, for six months. After completing the course of study, he or she is then assigned to a band. If qualified, he or she can also choose to continue studying advanced courses in conducting, composing, and arranging. The training facility is on the same level as a civilian conservatory, and it is recognized and accredited as such. The government will also pay tuition costs for those who wish to continue studying on their own time at a local college or university.

Depending upon an individual's instrumental skill and musicianship and the band he or she is joining, the starting grade is E-3, and can be E-4, E-5, or E-6, which is higher than the regular recruits, and the salary and working conditions are comparable to civilian occupations. Benefits include a thirty-day vacation, full medical care, commissary and post exchange privileges, as well as pension and retirement benefits.

There is a need for good musicians and singers in the military, especially woodwind and horn players. With the incentives that are being offered, it might be worth your while to examine the possibilities. Your local recruiter should have a video and information showing the opportunities available for musicians in that particular branch of the service. Openings for instrumentalists and vocalists are advertised in the *International Musicians' Journal.* In rare cases, an assignment with a special band does not require basic training or attending the military school of music.

For information see your local recruiter or write to the following addresses:

Navy

Navy Music Program Management Division

PERS-64
Navy Personnel Command
5720 Integrity Drive
Millington, TN 38055-6400
bupers.navy.mil/navymusic

Army

The U.S. Army Band

Public Affairs Office
204 Lee Avenue, Building 400
Fort Myer, VA 22211-1199
army.mil/armyband

Air Force

Air Force Bands Division (SAF/PAB)

Public Affairs Resource Library
1690 Air Force Pentagon
Washington, D.C. 20330-1690
af.mil/band

Marines

United States Marine Band
Director
Marine Barracks
Eighth and I Streets SE
Washington, D.C. 20390-5000
marineband.usmc.mil

Coast Guard

U.S. Coast Guard Band
U.S. Coast Guard Academy
15 Mohegan Avenue
New London, CT 06320
www.cga.edu/band/cgbandrecruiting.html

9

More Music Business

Agents

Booking agencies come in various sizes, from a local one-agent operation to the large national firms that maintain offices in many cities, a large staff of agents, and departments that cover all the categories in show business. An agent generally receives a commission of 10 percent or 15 percent, depending upon the situation.

It takes an agent more time and energy to book a $100 act than it does to book a $10,000 act, and since most agents already have a roster of artists and a circuit of clubs they book, it's not easy for them to take a chance on an unknown. Usually, in the beginning stages of a performing career, an artist has to act as his or her own agent and manager—knocking on doors, showcasing, sending out publicity, working small clubs.

It takes time for an artist to build a reputation that an agent will have enough confidence in to book an act. As artists become more popular, they begin to get recognition from local agents, and then, through the same self-motivation and persistence, they will get the larger agencies to notice them.

The local yellow pages list agents under Theatrical Agents, Musicians, and Orchestras and Bands. Some agents advertise in the *International Musician*. Many agents are franchised in more than one of the unions: AFM, AFTRA, SAG, Actors' Equity, AGMA, or AGVA. Each of these unions maintains an agency list. The trade papers (*Variety*, *Backstage*, *Billboard*, *The Hollywood Reporter*, and *Daily Variety*) contain a lot of information about agents and bookings.

Personal Managers

A personal manager is the one who is responsible for all the planning and strategies involved with developing an artist's career. A personal manager is involved with contract negotiations, record companies, publicity, bookings, and even solving personal problems.

In the case of the artist who earns a lot of money, a business manager generally handles investments, accounting, and taxes. The artist and manager must have a good personal relationship and a mutual trust for each other since a manager generally has power of attorney. Some managers charge a flat fee, and others have a sliding fee with a maximum cut-off point. Fees can range from 15 percent to 50 percent of the gross, and all expenses are usually paid by the artists.

Like the agent, a manager can't make money from an act that doesn't command large fees. However, unlike the agent, a manager who can recognize talent and an artist's potential will sometimes work at developing an unknown artist into a star.

Performers who go on a concert tour need a whole cast of support personnel to get that show on the road. That includes the road manager, stage manager, roadies, lighting and sound technicians, back-up musicians, and singers. All of these support personnel are learning their trade from the road up. This valuable on-the-job training can lead any of them into careers as concert promoters, personal managers, booking agents, producers, and even artists.

Organizations that have a membership of personal managers are:

National Conference of Personal Managers (East and West)
46–19 220th Place
Bayside, NY 11461-3654

Nashville Association of Talent Directors
P.O. Box 23903
Nashville, TN 37202-3903
n-a-t-d.com

Billboard's *2000 International Talent and Touring Directory* lists thousands of booking agents, personal managers, public relations firms, and business management firms. A list of personal managers also is published in the *Film and Television Directory* (Peter Glenn Publications, pgdirect.com).

Arts Managers

Arts managers represent instrumentalists, vocalists, conductors, orchestras, ensembles, and dancers in the field of serious music. An arts manager in this field not only books the artist but also develops the artist's career. A manager is generally responsible for many details when coordinating a booking, such as promotion, transportation, advertising, ticket sales, and accommodations. For information write:

The Association of Performing Arts Presenters
1112 Sixteenth Street NW, Suite 400
Washington, D.C. 20036
www.artspresenters.org

Arts Administrators

Arts administrators manage and run symphony orchestras, opera companies, and community arts projects. The general manager is responsible for the entire staff, which includes fund-raising, public relations, program planning, library, and ticket sales. Many musicians have found careers in management and administration preferable to a career in performing.

Many schools have courses and degree programs for performing arts management. Some subjects taught in such schools are concert promotion, talent booking and management, market research, administration of performing arts organizations, labor relations, public relations, grant proposal writing, and government and community resources.

Piano Tuners/Technicians

It is estimated that there are more than ten million pianos in this country—nine million in private homes and one million in schools and entertainment facilities. According to the Bureau of Labor

Statistics, in 1998 approximately thirteen thousand people worked as piano tuners and instrument repair technicians. Approximately two-thirds of all tuners are self-employed. The rest work for school systems, music stores, and piano manufacturers. It also reported that 50 percent of all tuner/technicians have a bachelor's degree.

To tune a piano, the pitch of the 'A' string (440 pitch) is adjusted by turning the pin with a tuning hammer (which is really a wrench) until it matches the pitch of the tuning fork. All the other strings are adjusted in relation to the 'A' string. The tuner's ear is trained to listen for the interfering sound waves, or beats, as he or she pulls each string into pitch.

The hammers wear out from constant use, so the tuner files them smooth again. After filing, the hammers have to be voiced and the action regulated to take up the slack.

The tuner/technician carries special tools for repairing and replacing worn or broken parts and strings. Since the majority of work is done in private homes, the working conditions are pleasant; however, a tuner/technician must have a good personality and a good appearance in order to deal with the public successfully. It takes approximately one to two hours to tune a piano.

Although there are a lot of pianos in homes, it doesn't represent that much work. Most people tend to neglect regular maintenance, especially in bad economic times, and some avoid it completely. In hotels, schools, opera companies, and clubs, the pianos are usually tuned once a week.

Most tuners get their training on the job by working under the guidance of an accomplished tuner/technician. It takes about two to five years to become a fully qualified tuner. There are some schools that offer courses in tuning and maintenance, as well as home study correspondence courses. A partial list is available from the Piano Technician's Guild. There are also special schools for the blind and visually handicapped.

A self-employed tuner can charge from $40 to $100 a tuning. Some technicians who are also good at woodworking specialize in rebuilding and refinishing pianos, and the profits from that add to their incomes. According to the Bureau of Labor Statistics, median annual earnings of musical instrument repairers and tuners were $23,010 in 1998. The middle 50 percent earned between $17,780 and $29,500 a year. The lowest 10 percent earned less than $13,230 and the highest 10 percent earned more than $38,680 a year. Earnings are generally higher in urban areas. There is also a need for technicians to tune and repair electronic and pipe organs in churches, synagogues, auditoriums, theaters, schools, and private homes. And with today's new technology, technicians are also needed to repair synthesizers, samplers, electric pianos, and amplifiers. A musician with a knowledge of electronics, who can also handle a soldering iron, should examine the possibilities of working in electronic instrument repair. For more information write:

Piano Technicians Guild
3930 Washington
Kansas City, MO 64111-2963
ptg.org

Manufacturing and Sales of Instruments

There are many opportunities for musicians in this area of the business—musicians who are willing to combine their talents with other skills such as marketing, sales, repairing, designing, and handcrafting. Every instrument and accessory has to be invented and designed.

Not only new but also the standard instruments need improvements, new materials, and techniques. That calls for research and development engineers. And who would know better than a musician what sounds, feels, and plays better on her or his instrument? The ability to play several instruments is a big asset to an inventor.

A musician who has been influenced by the age of electronics and whose curiosity has led to the understanding of computers, chips, and circuitry is standing on the threshold of electronic instruments—the invention and design and also the building, testing, repairing, demonstration, selling, and performing of these instruments.

A musician who is good at woodworking and finishing can turn to building guitars, violins, cellos, pianos, and other stringed instruments. Musicians who enjoy working with metal—soldering, shaping, plating, and machining—can also find careers in building brass instruments.

Every instrument built needs to be inspected and tested, and that takes someone with a thorough knowledge of the instrument and music. Many instrument manufacturers have training programs so that a musician can gain experience on the job. In some cases, after gaining experience, a musician can also build instruments in her or his own shop. Other opportunities in manufacturing are management, sales, product development, promotion, advertising, and demonstrating.

Musical Instrument Repair Technicians

A musician who can diagnose problems and repair instruments is always in demand. Musical instrument technology courses at colleges and universities can prepare someone for a career in woodwind, brass, string, and percussion repair. A repair person can also own and operate her or his own repair shop. The shop could include instrument and sheet music sales, as well as private instruction.

The Purchaser's Guide to the Music Industries is a journal that has information on manufacturers of musical instruments, industry associations, industry schools, the Canadian music industry, keyboard manufacturers, and much more. For information write:

The Guitar and Accessories Marketing Association
262 West Thirty-eighth Street, Room 1506
New York, NY 10018
www.discoverguitar.com

The Music Distributors Association (MDA)
262 West Thirty-eighth Street, Room 1506
New York, NY 10018
www.distributors.org

The Music Trades
80 West Street
Englewood, NJ 07631
musictrades.com

National Association of Band Instrument Manufacturers (NABIM)
262 West Thirty-eighth Street, Room 1506
New York, NY 10018
nabim.org

The Percussion Marketing Council
262 West Thirty-eighth Street, Room 1506
New York, NY 10018
playdrums.com

The National Association of Music Merchants (NAMM), a.k.a. International Music Products Association, promotes the study and growth of music markets, the enhancement of equitable and constructive legislation, training for members and their employees, developing technicians for the servicing of music products, researching, gathering and organizing industry statistics, and conducting trade shows, educational exhibits, and national meetings for all its members. NAMM also maintains a Management and Sales Training Institute. NAMM along with VH-1, located at vh1.com; the National Academy of Recording Arts and Sciences (NARAS), www.grammy.com; the American Music Conference (AMC), found at amc-music.com; the National Association for Music Education (MENC), www.menc.org; the National Schools Board Association (NSBA), www.nsba.org; and other groups promote music education in the schools through their "Save the Music"campaign. For more information contact:

International Music Products Association

National Association of Music Merchants (NAMM)
5790 Armada Drive
Carlsbad, CA 92008
namm.com

The National Association of Professional Band Instrument Repair Technicians (NAPBIRT)

P.O. Box 51
Normal, IL 61761
napbirt.org

Minnesota State College Southeast Technical offers a band instrument repair program. The credits earned can be applied to a baccalaureate degree. For information and a bulletin, contact:

Minnesota State College Southeast Technical

308 Pioneer Road
Red Wing, MN 55066-9951

Bibliography

Brochures and Books

Careers in Music

American Music Conference (brochures, videos, books), 5790 Armada Drive, Carlsbad, CA 92008-4608, amc-music.org.

Careers in Music (video and brochure). Music Educators National Conference, 1806 Robert Fulton Drive, Reston, VA 20191, menc.org.

Careers with Music. Incorporated Society of Musicians, 10 Stratford Place, London, W1C1AA, United Kingdom.

Ellis, Elmo I. *Opportunities in Broadcasting*. Lincolnwood, IL: VGM Career Books, 1998.

Moore, Dick. *Opportunities in Acting Careers*. Lincolnwood, IL: VGM Career Books, 1998.

"Music Makes the Difference: Music, Brain Development, and Learning." The National Association for Music Education

(MENC), 2000. 1806 Robert Fulton Drive, Reston, VA 20191.

Music Business and Copyrights

Baskerville, David, Ph.D. *Music Business Handbook and Career Guide*. Thousands Oakes, CA: Sage Publications, 2000.

Brabec, Jeffrey, and Todd Brabec. *Music, Money & Success*. New York: Gale Group, 2000.

Churchill, Sharal. *The Indie Guidebook to Music Supervision for Films*. Los Angeles: Filmic Press, 2000.

Music Business Directory, 1996. La Costa Music Business Consultants, P.O. Box 147, Cardiff, CA 92007, lacostamusic .com.

Shemel, Sidney, and William Krasilovsky. *This Business of Music*, 8th ed. New York: Watson-Guptill Publications, Inc., 2000.

Weissman, Dick. *The Music Business*. New York: Crown Publishing Group, 1997.

Composing, Musicianship, Film, and Conducting

Bell, David. *Getting the Best Score for Your Film*. Los Angeles: Silman-James Press, 1994.

Forsyth, Cecil. *Orchestration*. Mineola, NY: Dover Publications, 1989.

Ghezzo, Marta Arkossy. *Solfege, Ear Training, Rhythm, Dictation and Music Theory*. Tuscaloosa, AL: University of Alabama Press, 1994.

Kennan, Kent Wheeler, and Donald Grantham. *The Technique of Orchestration*. New York: Prentice Hall/Simon & Schuster Trade, 1996.

Mancini, Henry. *Sounds and Score*. Miami, FL: Warner Brothers Publications, 1995.

Persichetti, Vincent. *Twentieth-Century Harmony*. New York: W.W. Norton & Co., Inc., norton.com, 1961.

Rimsky-Korsakov, Nikolay. *Principles of Orchestration*. Mineola, NY: Dover Publications, 1990.

Rudolf, Max. *The Grammar of Conducting*, 3rd ed. New York: Schirmer Books, 1995.

Scherchen, Herman. *Handbook of Conducting*. Translated by D. Calvocoressi. New York: Oxford University Press, 1990.

Sebesky, Don. *The Contemporary Arranger*. Van Nuys, CA: Alfred Publishing Co., 2000.

Williams, Charles. *The Nashville Numbers System*; guitarnotes .com/alan/ah_nashville_numbers.

Songwriting

Boyce, Tommy. *How to Write a Hit Song, and Sell It.* North Hollywood, CA: Wilshire Book Company, mpowers.com, 1974.

Hall, Tom T. *The Songwriters Handbook*. Nashville TN: Rutledge Hill Press, rutledgehillpress.com, 1987.

Whitfield, Jane Shaw. *Songwriters Rhyming Dictionary*. North Hollywood, CA: Wilshire Book Company, mpowers.com, 1975.

Writers Digest Books. *Songwriters Market*. Cincinnati, OH: F&W Publications, Inc., writersdigest.com, 2002.

Recording

Hurtig, Brent. *Multi-Track Recording for the Musician.* Van Nuys, CA: Alfred Publishing, alfredpub.com, 2000.

Massey, Howard C. *The MIDI Home Studio.* New York: Music Sales Corporation, 1991.

Rapaport, Diane S. *How to Make and Sell Your Own Recording: A Complete Guide for Independent Labels.* Paramus, NJ: Prentice Hall, prenhall.com, 1999.

Runstein, Robert E., and David M. Huber. *Modern Recording Techniques.* Woburn, MA: Butterworth-Heinemann, 2001.

Trade Papers, Journals, and Magazines

Backstage

770 Broadway, 6th Floor
New York, NY 10003
backstage.com

Billboard

770 Broadway, 6th Floor
New York, NY 10003
billboard.com

Downbeat

Maher Publications
102 North Haven Road
Elmhurst, IL 60126
downbeat.com

Electronic Musician
Intertec Publishing Corp.
6400 Hollis Street, Suite 12
Emeryville, CA 94608
emusician.com

Film Music Magazine
350 North Glenoaks Boulevard, Suite 201
Burbank, CA 19502
filmmusicworld.com

Film Score Magazine
8503 Washington Boulevard
Culver City, CA 90232
filmscoremonthly.com

Guitar Player
Miller Freeman Inc.
411 Borel Avenue, Suite 100
San Mateo, CA 94402
musicplayer.com/guitarplayer

Guitar World
Harris Publications
1115 Broadway, 8th Floor
New York, NY 10010
musicplayer.com/guitarplayer

The Hollywood Reporter
5055 Wilshire Boulevard, 6th Floor
Los Angeles, CA 90036-4396
hollywoodreporter.com

International Musician
American Federation of Musicians
1501 Broadway, Suite 600
New York, NY 10036
afm.org

Keyboard
2800 Campus Drive
San Mateo, CA 94403
musicplayer.com

Mix Magazine
6400 Hollis Street, Suite 12
Emeryville, CA 94608
mixmag.com

Modern Drummer
Modern Drummer Publications, Inc.
12 Old Bridge Road
Cedar Grove, NJ 07009
moderndrummer.com

Music Books Plus
musicbooksplus.com
(formely *Mix Bookshelf*)

Musician
BPI Communications
770 Broadway, 6th Floor
New York, NY 10003
billboard.com

Opera News
Metropolitan Opera Guild, Inc.
70 Lincoln Center Plaza
New York, NY 10023
operanews.com

SHOOT Magazine
770 Broadway, 6th Floor
New York, NY 10003
billboard.com or bpicomm.com

Symphony Magazine
American Symphony Orchestra League
33 West Sixtieth Street
New York, NY 10023-7905
symphony.org

Variety
5700 Wilshire Boulevard
Los Angeles, CA 90036
variety.com

Variety
245 West Seventeenth Street
New York, NY 10011
variety.com

Directories

Amusement Business Publications
(theme parks, auditorium, and arena)
amusementbusiness.com

Backstage Performers Resource Service Directory
backstage.com

Billboard Publications
770 Broadway, Sixth Floor
New York, NY 10003
billboard.com or bpicomm.com
SHOOT Commercial Production Directory
International Music Industry Buyer's Guide
International Talent and Touring Directory
International Tape and Disc Directory

Broadcasting Yearbook, 2001
R.R. Bowker
630 Central Avenue
New Providence, NJ 07974

Music Business Register
7510 Sunset Boulevard, #1041
Los Angeles, CA 90046-3411
musicregistry.com

Musical America International Directory of Performing Arts
musicalamerica.com

National Association of Schools-of-Music Directory and Handbook
11250 Roger Bacon Drive, Suite 21
Reston, VA 20190
artsaccredit.org

Peter Glenn Publications
pgdirect.com
Fashion and Print Directory
Screen and Stage Directory
Film and Television Directory